# iCare™

## GRIEF MINISTRY GUIDE

**FOR CHURCH
LEADERSHIP AND CONGREGANTS**

INTERNATIONAL GRIEF INSTITUTE, LLC
COPYRIGHT © 2020

iCare Grief Ministry Guide– 1st ed.
International Grief Institute, LLC
www.InternationalGriefInstitute.com

Cover Design by AlyBlue Media, LLC
Interior Design by AlyBlue Media LLC
Published by AlyBlue Media, LLC
Copyright © 2020 by AlyBlue Media All rights reserved. No part of this publication may be reproduced, distributed or transmitted in any form or by any means, without prior written permission of the publisher.

ISBN: 978-1-950712-11-3
AlyBlue Media, LLC
Ferndale, WA 98248
www.AlyBlueMedia.com

This manual is designed to provide an informative grief support group format. It is sold with the understanding that the International Grief Institute is not engaged to render any type of psychological, legal, or any other kind of professional advice, nor does it authorize facilitators to do so. Neither the publisher nor the International Grief Institute shall be liable for any physical, psychological, emotional, financial, or commercial damages including but not limited to special, incidental, consequential or other damages should a facilitator or support group participant render advice on their own accord.

**PRINTED IN THE UNITED STATES OF AMERICA**

# CONTENTS

| | |
|---|---|
| **FOREWORD** | v |
| **PREFACE** | vii |
| **INTRODUCTION** | 1 |
| **CHAPTERS** | |
| Process of reconciliation | 13 |
| Communicating with family & friends | 21 |
| Confronting vs escaping grief | 29 |
| Caring for yourself | 33 |
| Anger | 39 |
| Guilt | 45 |
| Spiritual Lessons & Reconciliation | 51 |
| Turning pain into purpose | 59 |
| **RESOURCES** | 91 |
| **ACKNOWLEDGMENTS** | 101 |

# FOREWORD

**The Bible is for healing, sustenance and guidance.**

BY REV. ROLAND H. JOHNSON III

I have read and studied the texts and teachings of every major and many minor religions of the world. I have carefully and thoughtfully approached each with an open mind, without prior judgement or assumption. I believe the Bible, especially in the Hebrew and Greek texts, is the most complete and descriptive path for a life of truth, enlightenment, inner peace, contentment, joy and success.

To know yourself and use the gifts granted by divine authority of His Spirit, you must know the natural and the supernatural God. You must know forgiveness. You can learn to experience God's peace in your life.

Grief is the hardest work known to humans. As a disciple, you have the power to support the hearts of your bereaved in a meaningful way. As you proceed through the grief ministry training, please encourage those experiencing profound loss in your church and community to seek comfort and understanding from one another as well as in the Bible every day. Encourage them to "eat" scripture, "digest" it fully and slowly, and assimilate its truth and teaching into the body of their souls so they can grow in spirit and truth as they learn to move forward after loss.

The ICare Grief Ministry Guide is for those individuals who wish to reach out to friends, officemates, relatives, church members and others who have suffered the profound loss of a loved one. Based in a basic understanding of grief, this guide is intended as simple instruction to providing comfort, support, assistance, and faith.

Socially, most people today are not adept at dealing with death or the bereaved. Wanting to help, but fear of harm, stops many from doing anything or reaching out. Through understanding, you can reduce the fear of saying or doing the wrong thing and be more confident in your grief support.

Though you can learn on you own, we encourage the use of this book and the available ICare Grief Ministry Guide Workbook and other International Grief Institute resources to train support teams and a support network in your church or community organizations. If your church desires, IGI certified grief specialist are available to teach and train clergy, staff, leadership or congregants of your church or organization. Online coursework is available as well through the IGI website

We encourage the grief support groups in your church, organization, or on your own. IGI provides certified training for group facilitators, as well as the ICare Grief Support Group Facilitators Manual, and the ICare Grief Group Participants Manual. We would like to offer our support and expertise as you seek to educate and encourage the growth of good, competent grief support resources in your area.

Peace and blessings,

REV. ROLAND H. JOHNSON III

> **Thus says the LORD: "Stand by the roads, and look, and ask for the ancient paths, where the good way is; and walk in it, and find rest for your souls.**
> JEREMIAH 6:16 (ESV)

> **Your words were found, and I ate them, and your words became to me a joy and the delight of my heart, for I am called by your name, O LORD, God of hosts.**
> JEREMIAH 15:16 (ESV)

# PREFACE

**The Lord is close to the brokenhearted, and saves those who are crushed in spirit.**

PSALM 34:18

Griefwork—learning to live with a loved one in our heart instead of our arms—is a process of reconciliation, and the hardest work we'll ever do. It can strip our souls bare and leave us struggling for hope. The iCare Grief Ministry program equips disciples, facilitators and participants with useful and relevant tools that will support them as they begin to understand the reconciliation process.

Based upon balance, the program encourages participants to nourish their spiritual, physical and emotional selves along with strategies to help strengthen natural, inner resilience. Tending to their own needs now will serve them years down the road. They will learn to lead by example and become the light of hope for those behind them.

Though the physical absence of our loved ones will always be keenly felt, loss and grief are a classroom through which we learn life's most valuable lessons. Love, support, God's word, and nurturing of our emotional, physical and spiritual selves can make all the difference between surviving and thriving. That's what the iCare Grief Ministry program is all about.

LYNDA CHELDELIN FELL & LINDA FINDLAY
International Grief Institute

# INTRODUCTION

**So I exhort the elders among you, as a fellow elder and a witness of the sufferings of Christ, as well as a partaker in the glory that is going to be revealed: shepherd the flock of God that is among you, exercising oversight, not under compulsion, but willingly, as God would have you; not for shameful gain, but eagerly; not domineering over those in your charge, but being examples to the flock.**

1 PETER 5:1-3 (ESV)

## YOUR CHURCH AND A GRIEF MINISTRY

The iCare Grief Ministry program is designed to assist you in building, expanding or enhancing a comprehensive grief outreach for your church and community that will provide participants with comfort, understanding, and gentle guidance from both the Biblical standpoint as well as applied experience when faced with losing someone they love.

A comprehensive grief ministry in a church has three major components. First, pastors and staff trained in loss, grief, mourning and compassionate care are an essential part of grief ministry. Second, the pastor and staff require an understanding, loving and well-trained membership who is also knowledgeable in loss, grief, mourning and how to comfort the bereaved. Thirdly, development of **grief support groups** with skilled and **well-trained facilitators** are essential to a healing, supportive grief ministry.

## ICARE GRIEF SUPPORT GROUP FACILITATOR MANUAL

The iCare Grief Support Group program is designed to provide participants with comfort and gentle guidance from both the Bible standpoint as well as applied experience. The program is divided into eight sessions, each one carefully and thoughtfully designed to include the following key components:

- ✓ Discussion topic
- ✓ Helpful handouts
- ✓ Bible-based assignments
- ✓ Self-care tips
- ✓ Spiritual journaling

At the conclusion of all eight sessions, each participant will have had an opportunity to share and discuss common grief challenges, explore comforting scripture, compile a self-care plan, engage in spiritual journaling, and form lasting relationships and a network of support as they continue their individual journeys.

The iCare Grief Support Group Facilitator Manual includes everything you need to run a support group including instructions, forms, handouts, assignments, recommended readings, Resilience Rx™ self-care tips, and more. The support group format is designed to run as an 8-session program but can be easily adapted to a monthly drop-in format if needed.

## IMPORTANCE OF GRIEF SUPPORT GROUPS

Grief impacts and disrupts many areas of our lives. Without caring support, grief can impair a person's ability to move forward. Starting a grief Ministry Training is a rewarding experience. A good ministry training is multifaceted. The iCare Grief Support Group is designed to:

- ☑ Offer a supportive environment for people to work through their emotions and talk about their loved one.
- ☑ Introduce people to others who are going through a similar experience.
- ☑ Offer opportunities to learn new ways of coping with situations by listening to the experiences of other participants.
- ☑ Offer a chance to chat, laugh, and learn that the heart can hold joy and sorrow at the same time.
- ☑ Provide relevant Bible scriptures that answer common questions.
- ☑ Encourage spiritual journaling.
- ☑ Encourage self-care.

Studies show that peer support is more effective over psychotherapy and has become the standard of care (International Critical Incident Stress Foundation, 2016). As peer support is only one stop on the overall continuum of care, it's important for group facilitators to have a solid understanding of grief and its impact in the lives of those facing loss.

Following are fundamentals of the grief process including types, reactions and triggers. While there are commonalities most of us share, each grief journey is a unique reconciliation process—one that includes disruption, transition, and learning to adapt to living without the physical presence of our deceased loved one. Depending on our personality, prior traumatic experiences, and the relationship we shared with our loved one, this reconciliation process can take years.

While we will always miss our loved one, it's important to give participants hope that one day it won't always feel this raw. As a facilitator, you can provide that hope using the tools offered both in the Bible and the iCare program. If you feel motivated to lead a grief support group, learn more at www.icaregriefsupport.com/supportgroups.

# What does the Bible say?

The suggested scriptures in the iCare Grief Ministry Guide are a starting point only. The Bible offers far more instruction and comfort than can be covered in the scope of these assignments. Please explore beyond the suggested scripture when you feel motivated to do so. Much wisdom and insight are gained through reading the Bible, meditating upon its words and praying to God for insight, wisdom and understanding.

### READ SCRIPTURE SLOWLY AND CAREFULLY FROM A TRANSLATION YOU UNDERSTAND

Think about what you read and reflect on the various levels of meaning and application. Remember, prayer is a conversation with God. It need not be formal. Express yourself to God and express what you feel. Even negative, confused or angry feelings are okay when you talk with the Lord.

### REMEMBER ALWAYS . . .

Through Christ, you are a child of God. You are granted the privilege of God's personal attention and care through both good times and bad.

In 2 Samuel 18 tells the story of the death of Absalom, a favored son of King David. Though Absalom had made war on King David, David did all in his power to protect his son from harm. The scriptures carry the deep grief and emotion of King David at losing a son. The Book of Psalms, attributed to David, shares many deep emotions, feelings and great wisdom about the process of grief and one's relationship to God.

The story of Jacob's loss of his favorite son, Joseph, told in Genesis 37, reveals the struggle with inconsolable grief. The story of the coming Christ, from Isaiah 53, tells of the purpose of God's Son, Jesus Christ, bearing our grief and transgressions on our behalf. The New Testament proclaims hope, promise, relief and salvation from the grief, pain and suffering that fills our life. The resurrection of Christ and the promise of eternal life with God is the ultimate statement of hope for all who have experienced death of a loved one.

1 Peter 2 reminds us vividly that as believers in Christ we compose a royal priesthood, priest to each other, guaranteed the promise of eternal life and bound to help one another through all trials and suffering of life. John 3 Shares Christ's words of salvation and recognition that he was sent by the Father and would Himself experience death.

### THE BIBLE IS . . .

The Bible is for instruction, inspiration and consolation. The wisdom it contains will teach you how you can personally walk the journey of grief, mourning and bereavement as you continue to live and grow in faith.

## BIBLE ASSIGNMENTS

The Bible contains many teachings that can be helpful during grief. Each lesson includes one Bible assignment that encourages participants to explore the Bible and find scriptures that comfort them. The Bible assignments also provide room in the workbook for participants to journal feelings and emotions. Spiritual journaling is a powerful healing modality that should be encouraged. When you are comfortable in relying on the Bible and its wisdom, you will be comfortable sharing that wisdom with those who need comfort.

# Grief 101

We have all grieved, read and studied from the perspective of grief. Grief is a normal reaction to loss. Its complexity impacts the physiological, sociological, psychological, and spiritual self. It's important to note the following:

- All trauma has a grief associated with it, but not all grief has a trauma associated with it.

- Less complex losses, such as loss of a job, result in less complex grief. Profound, traumatic losses such as the unexpected death of a loved one, creates a psychological crisis with long-lasting effects on one's ability to cope and function.

- Grief's biological response is predictable but our emotional response—based upon our own inner resilience, adverse childhood experiences, personality type, access to social support, and more—is unique to each of us.

## BIOLOGICAL RESPONSES

When emotional trauma occurs, it floods the brain with adrenaline, a response known as fight-or-flight syndrome. It's designed to feed the muscles energy for increased strength and speed in anticipation of fighting or running. In response, other parts of the brain are anesthetized. This causes time warp, tunnel vision, and memory loss. This is why we recall trauma events like a strobe light rather than a story.

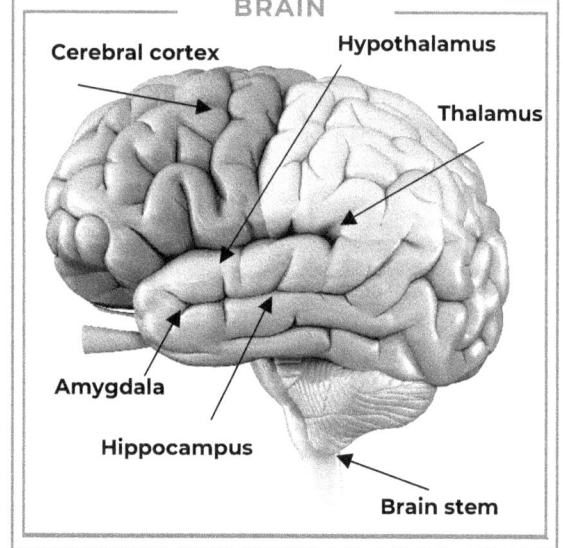

Biologically, the brain responds in a predictable pattern:

- **Brain stem** (the physical brain): Following a crisis, the brain stem is activated and the sympathetic nervous system sends the body into the fight, flight or freeze response. This involves over 120 different brain chemicals.

- **Limbic system** (the emotional brain): Second, the hippocampus, amygdala, and thalamus are stimulated. These structures regulate emotions, the storage of memories, and the interpretation of input from the senses. We remember the feelings associated with an event much more vividly than the details.

- **Cerebral cortex** (the thinking brain): The cerebral cortex is the least active part of the brain immediately following a crisis. Complex thinking such as problem solving and decision-making are somewhat impaired, and explains why people become confused and have a difficult time identifying options when in crisis.

## COGNITIVE AFFECTS

Psychologically, every event is interpreted through a number of filters unique to each person including:

- Physical proximity to the event
- Relational proximity to the event
- History of prior trauma
- Support system
- Personality

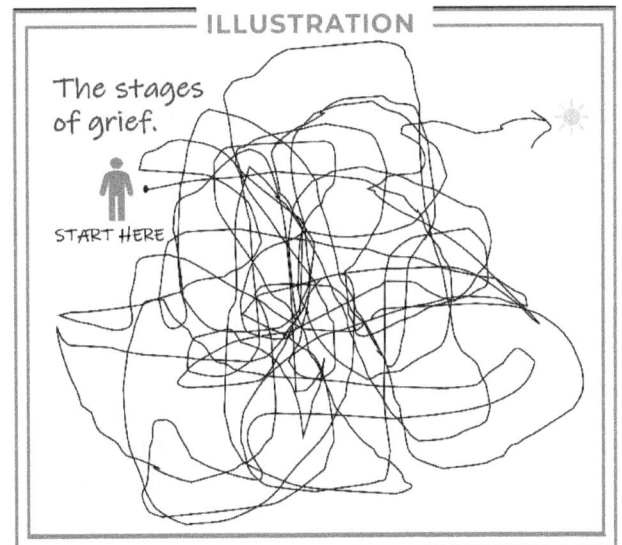

Cognitively, grief is a highly distracting process that diverts our emotional bandwidth and creates fears both rational and irrational. During the acute stage of grief, people are actively processing what happened. Healing begins in subsequent stages rather than right away.

Not all people respond the same way to death of a loved one. The emotional impact depends on a number of factors including inner resilience, personality, childhood experiences, and availability of support through family, friends, and coworkers. Some have more severe, longer-lasting reactions.

Lack of sufficient support can overwhelm a person's ability to cope and result in distress, impairment and dysfunction. Influencing factors also include:

- the extent of exposure to the event
- the amount of support during the loss event and its aftermath
- the amount of personal loss and social disruption

# Grief reactions

Though the nature and scope of grief differs, common reactions occur in 6 distinct categories.

- ☑ Cognitive
- ☑ Emotional
- ☑ Behavioral
- ☑ Physical
- ☑ Social
- ☑ spiritual

Understanding what are normal reactions is necessary to understand how to provide support.

**IMPORTANT**

**Any sign or symptom of abnormal reactions warrant referral to the next level of care. Refer whenever in doubt.**

## COGNITIVE REACTIONS

### NORMAL REACTIONS

- Forgetfulness
- Poor concentration
- Low productivity
- Negative Attitude
- Confusion
- Guilt
- Preoccupation with loss event

### ABNORMAL REACTIONS

- Suicidal/homicidal ideation
- Paranoid ideation
- Dissociation
- Disabling guilt
- Hallucinations
- Delusions
- Persistent helplessness

## BEHAVIORAL REACTIONS

### NORMAL REACTIONS

- 1000-yard stare
- Hyperstartle
- Sleep disturbance
- Crying spells
- Isolation
- Resentment
- Lashing out
- Increased risk-taking
- Distrust
- Withdrawal
- Impulsiveness
- Change in eating

### ABNORMAL REACTIONS

- Violence
- Antisocial acts
- Abuse of others
- Diminished personal hygiene
- Self harm
- Immobility
- Self medication

## EMOTIONAL REACTIONS

### NORMAL REACTIONS

- Anxiety
- Frustration and/or irritability
- Mood swings
- Temper outbursts
- Nightmares
- Crying spells

### ABNORMAL REACTIONS

- Panic attacks
- Immobilizing depression
- PTSD
- Depression
- Impaired functioning
- Infantile emotions

## PHYSICAL REACTIONS

### NORMAL REACTIONS

- Change in appetite
- Headaches
- Fatigue
- Insomnia
- Weight change
- Restlessness
- Upset stomach

### ABNORMAL REACTIONS

- Chest pain
- Irregular heartbeats
- Recurrent dizziness
- Recurrent headaches
- Collapse/loss of consciousness
- Numbness

**IMPORTANT**

All evidence of physical dysfunction should be taken seriously and referred to a physician, even if it seems ambiguous.

**IMPORTANT**

Physical complaints such as chest pain and breathing difficulty require immediate medical attention.

---

## SPIRITUAL REACTIONS

### NORMAL REACTIONS

- Emptiness
- Loss of meaning
- Doubt
- Unforgiving
- Looking for magic
- Loss of direction
- Cynicism
- Extreme or sudden religiousity
- Cessation from practice of faith

### ABNORMAL REACTIONS

- Religious hallucinations
- Religious delusions

## SOCIAL REACTIONS

**NORMAL REACTIONS**

- Upset in family
- Altered friendships
- Changes in workplace
- Altered status
- Role redefinitions
- Loss of motivation
- Loss of perspective
- Goal reorientation

**ABNORMAL REACTIONS**

- Withdrawal from all social contacts
- Quitting employment
- Total reassociation with antisocial groups
- Running away, disappearing

### RED FLAGS

Beyond intense physical complaints, there are 3 reactions that are never normal and are red flags for immediate evaluation:

- Suicidal thoughts with plan and intent
- Homicidal thoughts with plan and intent
- Hallucinations and/or delusions

It isn't uncommon for vague and fleeting suicidal thoughts to occur following death of a close loved one, but a formal mental health evaluation will help determine the danger level

# Grief types

Just as the grief journey is unique to each of us, there are also numerous types of grief. Below are the most common types you'll encounter when ministering to the bereaved.

### NORMAL GRIEF

A normal reaction to a loss event.

### ANTICIPATORY GRIEF

Grieving an anticipated death before it occurs, common when a loved one is dying from a terminal illness.

### TRAUMATIC GRIEF

Experiencing a sudden and unexpected loss; common when one has witnessed the actual death event.

### CUMULATIVE GRIEF

Experiencing a second loss while still grieving a prior loss. Also known as **grief overload**.

### COMPLICATED GRIEF

An ongoing, heightened state of mourning that is debilitating, and incapacitates on a long-term basis. It's a grief reaction that occurs when one fails to work through their loss, continually experiencing extreme distress with no progress towards feeling better and no improvement in day-to-day functioning.

### DELAYED GRIEF

Reacting much later to a death than is typical due to initial avoidance of the loss and emotional pain.

### MASKED GRIEF

A reaction that impairs normal functioning without the individual recognizing that the behaviors are related to the loss. Symptoms are often masked as either physical symptoms or other maladaptive behaviors.

### DISENFRANCHISED GRIEF

A rejection of one's mourning by their culture, family, social or work environment. The grief and suffering are disqualified by those around the mourner.

### ABSENT GRIEF

Reacting to a major loss by blocking one's feelings as though it never happened. The individual shows no reaction at all and fails to give it importance in his or her life.

## Grief triggers

Grief triggers are anything that brings up memories related to the loss and spark anxiety and/or emotional outbursts. Little reminders that throw us back in time and ambush emotions, they can happen anytime, anywhere, and be severe enough to induce a panic attack. If someone is struggling with severe triggers and panic attacks, encourage them to seek the care of their primary medical provider.

> **FACT**
>
> Triggers are a normal and common component of the grief process.

### TRIGGER EXAMPLES

- Spotting someone in the crowd who looks like our deceased loved one.
- The first flush of our deceased loved one's favorite flower.
- Scene of an accident.
- Sight of a hospital or favorite restaurant chain.
- Scent of loved one's cologne, perfume, flowers, food, etc.
- Sound of a song, train whistle, baby crying, horn honking, certain TV commercial, etc.
- A certain moment in time such as 11:30 p.m. when the original call came.
- Holidays, birthdays, anniversaries.

### WHAT TO KNOW

- People experiencing the same loss may not have the same triggers.
- Triggers may or may not lessen with time.
- Triggers can be subtle or surprising.

### HOW YOU CAN HELP

- Reassure them they're safe.
- Remind them to breathe.
- Avoid minimizing the trigger's significance even if you don't understand it.
- Hold the space for the mourner to work through it on their own.

## Caring Plan

Self-care is important when grieving a loved one. We can't always predict loss and other stressors, but practicing self-help techniques that tend to our physical, mental, emotional, and spiritual needs can help us cope. Encourage the bereaved to explore and utilize the Resilience Rx™ tips. The goal is to offer self-help strategies that trigger positive hormones—dopamine, serotonin, and oxytocin—to help support you and your participants as they learn to move forward with their loved one in their heart. Encourage the bereaved as they create their own caring plan.

## Compassion fatigue

Also known as **vicarious traumatization** or **secondary traumatic stress**, compassion fatigue is a cumulative physical, emotional and psychological effect of exposure to traumatic stories or events. It is emotional burnout attributed to the cost of caring for others. It occurs when we help others without recharging our own batteries.

As a grief support minister, it's important to be aware of compassion fatigue so you can guard against it. Below are common signs and management tips. If you feel an emotional burnout, it's important to share this with your church leadership. The longer you let it go, the harder it can be to recover from.

Your church has an invested interest in you taking care of both yourself and their congregants. You can't pour from an empty cup, nor would they want you to.

### COMPASSION FATIGUE SIGNS

- Emotional exhaustion
- Physical exhaustion
- Mental exhaustion
- Reduced sense of meaning in work
- Decreased interactions with others
- Irritability
- Inability to complete assignments and tasks
- Lack of flexibility
- Negativism

### MANAGEMENT

- Pray
- Stay hydrated
- Set emotional boundaries
- Practice good sleep hygiene
- Maintain a healthy work-life balance
- Use Resilience Rx™ strategies to recharge your own batteries

# CHAPTER 1

## PROCESS OF GRIEF RECONCILIATION

> Mourning is grief which is expressed to the outside world.

## Reconciliation of grief

### GRIEF VS MOURNING

Grief is an internal experience. For some, it is an inside fear, emptiness, panic, loneliness, anger, guilt, longing, or even depression. It's often expressed as, "Grief is love with no place to go."

Mourning is a bit different. It is the process where we work through our grief by outwardly expressing our internal feelings.

Grief without mourning is dangerous and destructive to the human system.

### WHEN GROWING UP, WHO TAUGHT US HOW TO MOURN?

All our lives, most of us have been taught how to acquire, not how to lose. Children and young adults are not offered a course in LOSS 101. No wonder it is strange and painful. Many mourn their grief as they witnessed a parent, movie or societal personality handle his or her grief.

As young people, we may have heard these messages:

- **"Don't feel bad, don't cry."**
  MESSAGE: Bury your feelings.

- **"You lost your toy! Well, just be good and Santa will bring another."**
  MESSAGE: Everything is replaceable.

- **"Now, you just keep your feelings to yourself."**
  MESSAGE: It isn't safe to share your feelings.

Who taught you how to experience loss and appropriately express feelings?

## GRIEF RECONCILIATION

Intellectually, you know you really don't recover from your grief in the sense that everything is restored to the way it was before. You know it's unlikely that life will ever be the same, yet at the beginning of our loss, this is difficult to accept.

You are beginning a process—a journey toward reconciliation—where you learn to adapt to living with your loved one in your heart.

## TASKS OF RECONCILIATION

There are a number of tasks ahead as you proceed with your own process of grief reconciliation.

- ✓ You learn to effectively experience and express outside of yourself the reality of the death.
- ✓ You allow yourself to fully embrace the pain of the loss, while learning how to assure that you are nurtured, physically, emotionally and spiritually.
- ✓ You learn to convert your relationship with the person who died from one of interactive presence to one of appropriate memory.
- ✓ You learn to develop a new self-identity based on a life without the person who died.
- ✓ You begin to relate the experience of the death to a context of new meaning in your life.
- ✓ You develop a lasting network of support to help you through the process.

In these next few weeks, you will learn safe ways to experience and express your grief.

- ✓ You will learn how to mourn while still taking care of yourself.
- ✓ You will begin to develop a new perspective about your loss and begin to clarify your self-identity.
- ✓ You will begin to discover a new sense of meaning in life while finding a network of supportive relationships to help you along the way.
- ✓ You are at an early stage of this process. Be patient and take it one moment at a time.
- ✓ Trust that it does get better. Because it does.

Learning to find the path for your personal reconciliation journey is what a support group program is are all about.

# SPIRITUAL JOURNALING

### KEEPING A SPIRITUAL JOURNAL

For the weeks ahead, you'll learn to keep a spiritual journal. Whether or not you choose to continue spiritual journaling once the training sessions are done, the writing you do in the coming weeks will be rewarding in ways you are unable to fully imagine now.

- ✓ Writing is a simple yet powerful way to help process your loss and work through your grief. It helps release some of the physical, emotional and spiritual pain that grieving folks experience.
- ✓ It will help you work through many of the issues that are difficult to communicate in other ways.
- ✓ It's very personal and confidential. Nobody needs to share in your journal writing unless you specifically choose to permit it. It is simple to do spontaneously.
- ✓ It does not require making complicated plans and can be accomplished right when your feelings and needs are strongest, even at 3 a.m.

### WRITE FOR YOURSELF

Even though we intellectually know that our own journal writing is for our eyes only, most of us have been conditioned differently. During school, we always wrote for others to see and usually judge, correct, and grade. At some point most of us have written a letter or two for someone else to read. Nearly all our prior writing has been to communicate with others.

### FOR YOUR EYES ONLY

While this sounds like an obvious thought, it can be difficult to grant ourselves permission to write freely without editorial judgement. As you progress in your writing, you will find that you are able to overcome the mindset that you are writing for others, and will concentrate on fully serving your own need for expression.

### HELPFUL HINTS

- ✓ Give yourself permission to write without perfection. God isn't looking for perfection.
- ✓ Use the pages of this book, a wide-lined school notebook, or one of those expensive designer journals. Give yourself permission to be as sloppy or as neat as you wish.
- ✓ Forget erasers. It is easier, quicker and more spontaneous to cross out words.
- ✓ There are no errors when writing for yourself, merely thoughts you wish to reread and those you want to skip. Rather than erasing or tearing out pages in order to obliterate, try putting a big X through a page or crossing out a phrase.
- ✓ Pay attention to those thoughts you are inclined to obliterate. Quite often they are a rich source of issues you need to work through in order to complete your griefwork.

- ✓ When staring at a blank page and unable to think of anything to say, write from your stream of consciousness.
    - Set a time limit. Start with maybe 5 to 10 minutes.
    - Write everything that comes into your mind, no matter how unconnected, scattered or inane it may seem.
    - Since we aren't judging ourselves and no one else will read it, it doesn't matter that it isn't a well composed sentence or paragraph. Capture whatever thought or image comes to mind.
    - Don't try to write a story. Merely begin to document your internal images, feelings, and internal dialogue.

Not having the pressure of composing something which makes sense, you just have to be able to write fast enough to keep up with your internal activity. If your thoughts lead to a particular issue, elaborate on it. When the allotted time has passed, you can choose to continue or allow yourself to stop for the day, and start fresh the next day.

You will surprise yourself at how quickly you have developed a new tool for making progress with your griefwork. With the mechanics of writing now a comfortable routine, you can become more focused.

In griefwork, we are frequently writing for one or more of the following reasons:

- ✓ To capture our experience or progress.
- ✓ To confront an issue.
- ✓ To vent, explore or express a feeling or emotion.
- ✓ To connect.
- ✓ To atone.
- ✓ To preserve a thought.
- ✓ To memorialize our loss.

### BENEFITS OF SHARING

While few people feel they want to share everything they've written, there is often therapeutic value in sharing some of it.

Some, in their writings, have discovered parts of themselves which they want to share. You are under no obligation to share, however, should you wish to, there is an opportunity to share during each support session.

### A TOOL FOR YOUR TOOLBOX

If writing has always been comfortable and easy, please continue to do it. If this is new to you, please ask for help and encouragement, as this is a useful tool that will serve you well even after you've done the largest portion of your griefwork.

# YOU & I

WHAT'S DIFFERENT ABOUT THESE TWO STATEMENTS?

**STATEMENT 1**

"When you ask someone for help time and time again, they are going to resent you. You feel real funny and you don't want to ask again. You get depressed after you try this a number of times and get no real help. What are you supposed to do? You just go on and on, and hope it will go away."

**STATEMENT 2**

"I find when I ask someone for help time and time again, they seem to resent me. I feel funny and I don't want to ask again. I get depressed after I try this a number of times, and I get no real help. What am I supposed to do? I just go on and on, and hope it will go away."

BOTH STATEMENTS ARE TRYING TO SAY THE SAME THING, EXCEPT . . .

In the first statement, we hear someone else telling us by implication how we should feel. If we don't feel that way, it can feel as though we're being told that we're strange and different, and may find ourselves inwardly resenting being grouped with that person's feelings.

The second statement is a direct report of someone else's experience, and leaves it up to us to choose whether or not we associate with it. It gives us permission to listen to it, and choose how we feel:

1. "Yes, I feel the same way. This is also my experience."
2. "No. I can understand how you may feel the way you do, but what you say does not relate to me and my experience."

In groups, it is important that members relate their direct experience and take full ownership and responsibility for their statements. This is best done through the use of **I** statements.

- I have no right to tell someone, "When so and so happens, you feel this way."
- I have every right to say, "When so and so happens, I feel this way."

In the normal conversational vernacular, the **you** means of expression is frequently used. However, in self-help groups where reports of direct individual experience are frequently so helpful, the use of **I** statements becomes more and more important.

We realize how difficult it is for some to reorient their habitual form of expression. Please don't get upset if you're interrupted with a gentle request to change your expression from a **you** statement into an **I** statement.

## COMMON FEELINGS

You have undoubtedly heard the term **grief work**. You may also have heard that the only way **out** is **through**. This means that avoidance of griefwork and the bereavement process only postpones your reconciliation. During the coming lessons you have an opportunity to learn new ways of working through grief, getting a better understanding of yourself and how to dissipate the strong feelings in healthy ways.

Many people come to support groups thinking there is something wrong with them. They are experiencing thoughts and emotions with an intensity they never thought possible. For some, the intensity causes them to feel as though they're going crazy, are out of control, and wonder whether the rollercoaster will ever stop. It will.

### YOU ARE NOT CRAZY

Following is a list of feelings and conditions which are common and normal during grief. You might experience many of these, or just a few. Much of a support group's time will be spent on how to recognize and deal with these feelings, their frequency and their intensity. Although normal, these feelings are still painful. Support sessions are not going to take the pain away. Because you're concentrating on your griefwork, you may even find that the pain intensifies—that, too, is normal. But you will be rewarded by your griefwork as the tunnel forward becomes brighter.

- Anniversary obsessions
- Anxiety
- Confusion
- Crying and sobbing
- Denial
- Depression
- Disbelief
- Disorganization
- Dreams
- Drugs and/or alcohol
- Emptiness
- Anger and/or rage
- Fear
- Grief attacks
- Guilt
- Helplessness
- Holiday obsessions
- Physical illness
- Joy and guilt
- Loss of intimacy
- Loss feelings
- Mystical experiences
- Numbness
- Obsession with personal objects
- Panic
- Powerlessness
- Psychological changes
- Regrets
- Release
- Relief
- Rumination
- Sadness
- Search for meaning
- Searching
- Self-Focus
- Shock
- Sudden mood changes
- Suicide thoughts
- Survivor's guilt
- Time distortion

# What does the Bible say?

Blessed are those who mourn, for they shall be comforted.

MATTHEW 5:4

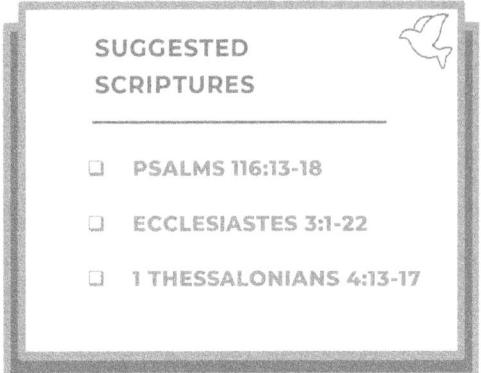

SUGGESTED SCRIPTURES

- PSALMS 116:13-18
- ECCLESIASTES 3:1-22
- 1 THESSALONIANS 4:13-17

The Christian view of death is special. The belief in God, resurrected Jesus, salvation, heaven and the eternity of the human spirit allows and encourages hope in time of despair.

In **2 Samuel 18** tells the story of the death of Absalom, a favored son of King David.

Though Absalom had made war on King David, King David did all in his power to protect his son from harm. The scriptures carry the deep grief and emotion of King David at losing a son.

The Book of Psalms, attributed to David, shares many deep emotions and feelings along with great wisdom about the process of grief and one's relationship to God.

Ecclesiastes speaks about the seasons of life. Much like the dead of winter is necessary for plants to regrow from the roots up, pain and sorrow often lead to necessary growth of our soul.

BIBLE ASSIGNMENT 1

## How does the Bible portray death? How do you feel about this?

**Does the Bible's portrayal of death bring you comfort? If so, what scriptures do you find helpful? Be prepared to discuss your answers at the next meeting.**

MY SCRIPTURES

ANSWER:

iCARE™ GRIEF MINISTRY GUIDE

# Caring Plan

RESILIENCE RX™ TIP 1
## Create your own

Losing someone we love changes how we live and who we are. The first step is to take good care of yourself. Self-care refers to healthy habits and activities that reduce stress and tend to your physical self.

*The love in the world begins with the love within ourselves.* DEEPAK CHOPRA

### WHY IT MATTERS

Grief is a significant stressor that impacts our emotional, mental and physical health. Self-care can improve our well-being, minimize stress, reduce the damaging effects of grief, and help us adjust as we learn to live with our loved one in our heart instead of our arms.

Creating a self-care plan that tends to your physical, emotional, social, and spiritual needs will help strengthen your inner resilience when juggling the demands of life while grieving, and can help anchor your ability to weather times of upheaval. By identify things you enjoy, you'll be able to create a unique and helpful self-care plan you'll stick with.

### PHYSICAL NEEDS

Nourishing your body will help you feel better. When you feel better, you cope better.

- Practice good sleep hygiene.
- Engage in light exercise, housekeeping or dancing to keep the body moving.
- Stay hydrated and eat for health.
- Make time for restorative relaxation.
- Enjoy a good belly laugh each day.

### SOCIAL NEEDS

Fulfilling engagements and interactions help guard against depression and isolation.

- Volunteer in the community.
- Take or teach a self-enrichment class.
- Join a book, tennis, quilt or knitting club.
- Travel.

### EMOTIONAL NEEDS

Emotional needs are met through understanding, empathy, and support.

- Surround yourself with others who speak your loss language.
- Develop supportive friendships.
- Talk to loved ones about your loss.
- Express your emotions in a journal.
- Engage in enjoyable activities.

### SPIRITUAL NEEDS

Spiritual needs are met through inner reflection.

- Each day write down one thing you're grateful for, or try spiritual journaling.
- Engage in reflective practices such as prayer or meditation.
- Try laughter yoga or forest therapy.
- Talk to clergy or a spiritual mentor.

# CHAPTER 2

## COMMUNICATING WITH FAMILY & FRIENDS

**Discuss how we are hurt by the ones we love.** What are some of the clichés and euphemisms we've heard?

- You must get a hold of yourself.
- Can't let yourself fall apart.
- Be strong, or be strong for the children.
- I know exactly how you feel.
- Well, at least s/he didn't suffer.
- It's over now. Let's talk about something pleasant.
- The living must go on living.
- S/he led a full life.
- Time will take care of it.
- God will never give you more than you can handle.

**What is happening when people use clichés and euphemisms?** Why do they do it?

- How do you handle these statements and ones like them?
- How do you feel about family or friends when they speak this way?
- How do you begin to forgive them?
- Do they really know what to say?
- Did you know what to say before you had your direct experience confronting the feelings you're living with?
- Are they afraid of our feelings? How do they feel about themselves?

Although well-intentioned, these statements often don't ring true. Perhaps all we want is for someone to really listen to us. Perhaps just want a simple honest expression of feelings, like:

- Could you tell me about it?
- What happened?
- I can't imagine how painful this must be.
- What was your relationship like?
- Simply saying "I'm so sorry," and then have them be quiet and listen to us.

We really have a choice about how to deal with folks who seem unable to deal with us. We can get angry, write them off, and never speak to them again. We can tell everyone else how insensitive they are. Or, we can choose to recognize that they just never learned how to deal with pain, and we can try to preserve the relationship by educating them.

## PLEASE LISTEN

When I ask you to **listen** to me
and you start giving advice
You really have not done what I asked.

When I ask you to listen to me and you begin to tell me why I shouldn't feel that way, my feelings feel trampled upon.

When I ask you to listen to me and you seem intent on solving my problems, you are failing me. Just listen.

All I ask is that you **listen**, please!
Don't **talk** or **do**, **just hear me**.

Advice is cheap. A quarter gets me both Dear Abbey and Billy Graham in the same newspaper, and I can do that for myself.

I'm not helpless.
Maybe discouraged and faltering,
but not helpless.

Please try to understanding. When you do something for me that I can and need to do for myself, rather than helping, you contribute to my fear and inadequacy.

When you accept as a simple fact that I really do feel the way I say I feel, no matter how irrational, then I can conserve my precious energy.

I then have the energy to get about this business of understanding what's behind my irrational feelings.

And when that's clear, the answers become obvious and the advice becomes unnecessary.
I can make sense of my irrational feelings when I begin to understand what's behind them.

**So please listen and just hear me**.

And if you want to or need to talk,
wait for your turn, and I'll **listen** to you.

# EMPOWERMENT

Some of us were brought up to merge our self with those around us: our family, our schools, churches and other social organizations.

Under the umbrella of family or group, we learned to subvert our interests and needs to others who were more powerful, such as a parent, older sibling, chronically ill family member, a school system, government, etc.

In marriage, some of us continued subverting our needs to our spouse, children and aging parents. Our own self may never have had the opportunity to fully develop. We never learned to exchange information and emotions with others while maintaining individuality.

We never learned to connect without merging, without loss of our own self.

When we overly identify with others, we lose our boundaries. When we set boundaries, we are honoring that part of us which makes us a unique and important individual.

Much of our unhappiness and worry results from our inability to set boundaries. We have learned not to feel empowered to be our own self. We haven't learned how to be oneself as a separate entity from someone else.

As a result, inside ourselves, sometimes barely conscious, our body system continues to deny its unique existence.

In the lessons, we begin to acknowledge our unique personhood. We may need to learn how to undo years of practice where we gave priority to the needs of others rather than consciously acknowledging our own.

In this process, we will be careful of extremes. We are not trying to establish walls. We are not looking for boundaries so rigid that they are no longer permeable.

However, we're going to learn how to acknowledge, validate, and give importance to our needs as humans.

## AFFIRMATIONS FOR EMPOWERMENT

- My emotions are allies
- I can heal
- I can trust
- I have resources
- I have boundaries
- I can experience intimacy
- My body belongs to me
- I have an unconscious
- I have a future

- I have inner guides
- My emotions are allies
- I can reject others
- I can release self-blame
- I can participate in a community
- I can enjoy my sexuality
- I can support and respect myself

## PLEASE SEE ME THROUGH MY TEARS

You asked me how I was doing. When I replied, tears came to my eyes.

You immediately began to talk again. Your eyes looked away, your speech picked up, and all the attention you had given me went away. How am I doing?

I do better when you will listen to my response, even though I may shed a tear or two, for I so want your attention. But to be ignored because I am in indescribable pain, that hurts me and makes me feel angry.

So, when you look away, I feel alone.

Really, tears are not a bad sign you know.

They're nature's way of helping me to heal. They relieve some of the stress of sadness.

I know you fear that asking me how I'm doing brought this sadness to me.

No, it didn't. The memory of my loss will always be with me, only a thought away. It's just that my tears make my pain more visible to you, but you did not give me the pain, it's just there.

When I cry, could it be that you feel helpless?

You're not, you know.

When I feel your permission to allow my tears to flow, you've helped me more than you can know.

You need not verbalize your support of my tears. Your silence as I cry is my key. Do not fear my tears.

Your listening with your heart to, "How are you doing," helps relieve the pain, because once I allow the tears to come and go, I feel lighter.

Talking to you releases things I've been wanting to say aloud,

and then there's space for a touch of joy in my life.

When I tear up and cry, that doesn't mean I'll cry forever, maybe just a minute or two, and then I'll wipe the tears away. Sometimes you'll find I'm even laughing at something funny ten minutes later.

When I hold back tears, my throat grows tight, my chest aches and my stomach begins to knot up, because I'm trying to protect you from my tears.

But then we both hurt. Me, because I've kept the pain inside and it's become a shield against our closeness. You hurt because we're now distant.

Please take my hand. I promise not to cry forever; it's physically impossible, you know.

When you see me through my tears, then we can be close again.

# COMPANIONS

### ACTIVE LISTENING

One of the most important things someone can do for a person in grief is to listen, because we need to tell our story over and over again.

The head knows what's happened but it takes a long time for the heart to catch up, and telling the story is the way that is accomplished.

People are often worried about what to say, and not knowing what to say is what keeps them away from us. "I don't know what to say. I might say the wrong thing."

But really, you need to say very little. Active listening is what will help me heal most.

### INTENSITY OF EMOTIONS

There are many emotions in grief, and the intensity of those emotions can be frightening. That's why people want to avoid grieving; it's hard work. Some of the hardest feelings are just plain sadness and feeling helpless.

We replay our loss again and again, trying to figure out whether we could have done something different. We always end up at the same point; there was nothing we could do.

Griefs that haven't been expressed never go away. They don't just disappear.

You have to grieve, you have to get it out. And if you don't, it's going to hurt you. It's going to hurt those around you, and it's going to affect you physically.

It's so important to get grief out. That's why we need people to listen to us.

### IDENTIFY YOUR FEELINGS

You need to say what you're feeling—and keep talking about it. Listeners can help us by giving us a safe place to talk about our loss and all the feelings that are part of it.

The process is different for everyone, but the initial period of grief often includes shock, numbness, and even feeling disconnected from our body and can be frightening.

> "I feel helpless."
>
> "I feel sad."
>
> "I feel angry."

Further along, you might obsess for your loved one, have dreams about him or her, think you saw or even heard them speak. These thoughts can make us feel crazy at times. It's frightening if you don't know that this is normal.

In another phase of the grief journey we often feel disorganized, physically depressed, and feel as though we're physically falling apart.

Eventually, things begin to normalize. We start to eat and sleep normally, and life starts to fit into a normal pattern that feels good enough to live with.

After the initial shock of grief wears off, you feel like other people don't want you around when you're feeling sad. Nobody likes to be sad, and nobody likes to be around sad people, so we hide.

It's hard going back to work, back to church, back to the office, back into a routine. If there's any one wonderful thing that a person can do to help a griever, it's to say "Come with me. I'll sit with you in church," or "Let's go together to the office today," or something like that.

You need someone to take your hand and help you back into your normal life—a companion along the way.

Adapted from a radio interview transcript with the Reverend Corrine Chilstrom, Associate Pastor at St. Luke's Lutheran Church in Park Ridge, IL., conducted by Richard A. Jensen, Director/Speaker of LUTHERAN VESPERS, a radio ministry of the Evangelical Lutheran Church in America, based upon Pastor Chilstrom's book: "Andrew, You Died Too Soon." The subtitle is "A Family Experience of Grieving and Living Again."

# What does the Bible say?

Rejoice with those who rejoice,
and weep with those who weep.

ROMANS 12:15

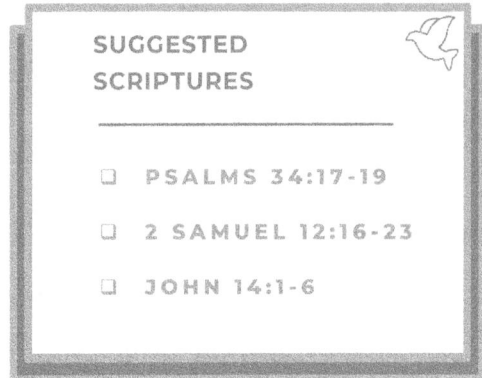

**SUGGESTED SCRIPTURES**

- PSALMS 34:17-19
- 2 SAMUEL 12:16-23
- JOHN 14:1-6

The story of Jacob's loss of Joseph, his favorite son, told in **Genesis 37**, reveals Jacob's struggle with inconsolable grief.

The story of the coming Christ, from **Isaiah 53**, tells of the purpose of God's Son, Jesus Christ, bearing our transgressions and grief on our behalf.

The New Testament proclaims promise, hope, relief and salvation from the grief, pain and suffering that fills our life. The resurrection of Christ and the promise of eternal life with God is the ultimate statement of hope for all who experience death of a loved one.

BIBLE ASSIGNMENT 2

## What does the Bible say about grieving the death of a loved one?

**Does the Bible's portrayal of grief and mourning bring you comfort? If so, what scriptures do you find helpful? Be prepared to discuss your answers at the next meeting.**

MY SCRIPTURES

ANSWER:

# Caring Plan

RESILIENCE RX™ TIP 2
## Sensorial Therapy

Our five senses play a role in how we feel and can be influenced by what our senses take in.

Practice the Rule of 5s below to give yourself some form of sensory pleasure every day. With practice, the awareness and perception of delight eventually becomes effortless, and is an important step toward restoring balance after loss.

A treat is a small pleasure that we give to ourselves. GRETCHEN RUBIN

**WHY IT MATTERS**

When grief overwhelms you, treat your five senses to things that look, feel, smell, taste, or sound good. Treating yourself to something that evokes sensorial joy stimulates the feel-good hormones in your brain to help offset the stress of grief.

---

**RULE OF 5s**

**Every day practice the Rules of 5 by enjoying the following:**
- ✓ 5 things you can see
- ✓ 4 things you can touch
- ✓ 3 things you can hear
- ✓ 2 things you can smell
- ✓ 1 thing you can taste

---

Find ways to stimulate your senses in pleasurable ways. In addition to stimulating your brain's feel-good hormones, research shows that certain actions such as coloring (sight) and foods (taste) also help reduce stress, including avocado, oatmeal, raspberries, blueberries, oranges, pistachios, walnuts, and chocolate.

# CHAPTER 3

## CONFRONTING VS ESCAPING GRIEF

**ESCAPING**

Our natural reaction as humans are to fight, flight or freeze—it's how our brain responds. While escape is sometimes appropriate, the only way to escape grief is to grieve. Therefore, the time comes when it is appropriate to confront our grief by outwardly mourning. We can easily put off facing the reality of our feelings maybe for days, weeks, months, years, or even a lifetime.

- We aren't really escaping, there is no escape; but we give an appearance of escape.
- By not confronting and working through the grief, the feelings may be ever present.
- If not in consciousness, they will work on our physical or emotional system, leading to sickness and disease.

**How do some of us escape our feelings?** In what ways are you escaping? Examples include:

- Addictions, work, prescription drugs, substance use, alcohol, inappropriate loving.
- Overeating or undereating.
- Activity frenzy through lots of travel and busyness.
- Isolating and avoiding situations where we need to talk about our feelings.

**CONFRONTING**

We need to deal with the reality of our feelings when we're ready to do so. This helps to relieve the physical and emotional self of the need to indefinitely carry the pain. How do we confront our feelings?

- Do some writing about our loss.
- Allow alone time to really **think** vs frantic busyness.
- Talk about feelings and loss with others.
- Consciously externalize (physically express) our feelings.
- Dispose of clothing and personal effects, if desired.

## What does the Bible say?

**SUGGESTED SCRIPTURES**

- ISAIAH 53:1-2
- ISAIAH 28:3-16
- HEBREWS 12:7-13

Our friend Lazarus sleeps, but
I go that I may wake him up.

JOHN 11:11

In the Bible, death is often referred to as sleep, a metaphor that emphasizes the fact that the first death is temporary. This understanding of death is much more comforting than all the unbiblical and erroneous ideas about death.

When someone dies, family and friends often suffer with regrets and feelings of guilt about things they said or did, or didn't say or do. God doesn't want us to beat ourselves up about the past. He wants us to look forward to the future he has in store for us, and our reunion in the next life when we'll have plenty of time to talk to our loved ones.

BIBLE ASSIGNMENT 3

## What does the Bible say about dealing with and managing grief?

**How do you feel about the scriptures you found on this? What scriptures do you find helpful? Be prepared to discuss your answers at the next meeting.**

**MY SCRIPTURES**

ANSWER:

# Caring Plan

RESILIENCE RX™ TIP 3

## Sleep well

Losing a loved one creates upheaval that can lead to many sleepless nights. Juggling such emotional strains often leads to serial tossing and turning, sleep disruption and insomnia. In turn, the ensuing sleep deprivation magnifies our emotions and reduces our ability to cope with the upheaval, creating what feels like an unending circle.

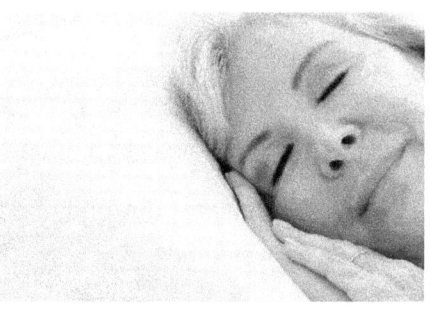

When you have laboriously accomplished your daily task, go to sleep in peace.
VICTOR HUGO

WHY IT MATTERS

Studies show that receiving less than 7 hours of sleep at night may increase our risk of diabetes, heart conditions, obesity, or anxiety. Managing sleep disruption and insomnia by practicing good sleep hygiene, coupled with medical management when needed, can help restore a restful sleep pattern after loss, and lead to significant improvements in other distress symptoms (National Institutes of Health, 2008).

> **CREATE A RITUAL**
>
> Create a relaxing bedtime ritual gives your mind and body time to wind down. It sends a signal to your brain that bedtime is near, and trains it to go into quiet mode.

BENEFITS OF GOOD SLEEP HYGIENE

Healthy sleep habits are an essential part of caring for yourself, and can make a big difference in your quality of life. Studies show that good sleep helps you cope better in times of stress. It can also lower your blood pressure, improve your memory, help keep your immunity strong, and puts you in a better mood.

Known as good sleep hygiene, healthy bedtime habits can influence the body's circadian rhythms. Healthy daytime habits, including what you eat, drink, how much daylight and physical exercise you get, also play roles.

## SLEEP HYGIENE TIPS:

Try the following suggestions from the National Sleep Foundation to help you reestablish a restorative sleep pattern after losing someone you love.

- To help regulate your body's clock, stick to a sleep schedule of the same bedtime and wake time, even on weekends.

- Exercise early in the day. Vigorous exercise is best, but even light exercise is better than no exercise.

- A sleep environment between 60 and 67 degrees is ideal.

- If your partner snores, consider using a fan, earplugs, or white noise.

- Use comfortable pillows and bed linen.

- Consider moving around the bedroom furniture, repainting the bedroom walls, and purchasing new bed linen.

- Avoid bright light in the evening to keep your circadian rhythm in check.

- Avoid alcohol, caffeine, cigarettes, and heavy meals later in the day.

- Try wearing a sleep mask or weighted blanket across your feet to help reduce stimuli and calm your mind.

If you continue to struggle with sleepless nights after trying the tips above, cognitive behavioral therapy is one of the top suggestions for treating long-term sleep disruption. Speak to your doctor to learn more about this process.

# CHAPTER 4

## CARING FOR YOURSELF

Grief can make us feel out of control. Self-care helps to restore some of that control through managing our health and well-being. When we feel physically and spiritually stronger, our coping improves.

**Physical**. How do you physically feel right now? Do you have any aches or pains? Do you feel physically strong or rundown? What measures do you take at home to ensure good health? Is there room for improvement? Suggestions for tending to your physical self:

- Exercise: Walking, yoga, swimming, jogging, biking, chop wood. What else can you do?
- Rest and relaxation. Picking a time to rest and relax your physical self.
- Nutrition: Regular eating times, balanced meals.
- Massage, Reiki, acupuncture, etc. Try it; maybe you'll like it.

**Emotional**. How do you emotionally feel right now? Do you feel strong or fragile? Do you feel alert, engaged, and aware of the world outside your own? Suggestions for tending to your emotional self:

- Become aware of your emotional being. Keep a journal of your feelings.
- Give yourself permission to express emotions. Holler, scream, cry, laugh.
- Find a friend who you can share anything with.

**Intellectual**. How do you feel intellectually? How do you care for your intellectual self? Suggestions for tending to your intellectual needs:

- Take a personal enrichment course.
- Read a book every month, any book. Just read.
- Play games or do puzzles.

**Spiritual**. How are you feeling spiritually? Not necessarily religious, but spiritual? Suggestions for tending to your spiritual needs:

- Walk a trail or take a trip to the mountain or beach.
- Book a retreat.
- Take a spiritual workshop or revisit the faith of your childhood.

# CONTROLLING STRESS WITH YOUR CALM SCENE

The day-to-day difficulties of modern society is a cause of stress. You may not be able to avoid or get rid of it, but you can learn to control it.

In your mind, create and visualize a feeling where you can experience a unique sense of peace, a oneness with the world. Some use a time when they recall being particularly connected with nature. Suggestions:

- On a mountaintop looking into the distant valley below, surrounded by silence
- At the seashore looking into the distant vastness of the ocean horizon

Some have associated **calm** with a single moment when, for an instant, they felt a certain peace or even absence of conflict, where there was a pause in the cares of the world and a sense of peace descended over them.

Whatever your unique visualization, there are certain guidelines to use in selecting a **calm scene** which will serve you as you continue on your journey.

### SPECIFIC SCENE:

- ❏ Select a scene where you are absolutely alone and safe. It should be a specific place, not a general or vague memory like "in the woods somewhere."
- ❏ To make your image clearer, use all your senses. What do you see? What do you hear? What do you smell? What do you feel?
- ❏ Your physical activity should be limited. Excessive activity tends to remove the aspect of calm you are looking for.
- ❏ No substances. Your remembrance of **calm**, in order to be useful in your journey, should not be influenced by drugs, alcohol or tobacco.
- ❏ Now that you have selected your **calm scene**, write a short paragraph to describe it. Describe where you are, what you see, what you hear, what you smell or taste, how you feel, and where in your body you have this feeling.
- ❏ Put it to use. Find a moment when you can relax and enter into your **calm scene**. Once you're there in that calm, serene space in your head, anchor it with a touch by clasping the fingers of one hand around the wrist of the other hand. Feel a gentle wave of calmness and peace surge through your mind and body.

*Whenever you need to reduce stress, clasp your wrist in the same manner to trigger your calm scene.*

# LIFE QUALITY INVENTORY CHECK

Grief can have a dramatic effect on our physical, emotional and spiritual systems. It can be difficult to bring these systems into balance, particularly so if we aren't fully clear about ourselves.

This inventory is worthless unless you are completely honest with yourself. You don't need to share your answers with anyone, so please be totally honest with yourself. This will help you clarify where you are and help you to establish goals for changes you may want to bring about. These questions also make excellent prompts for the confidential journal writing. Once you're clear on these topics, you may choose whether it will be helpful or appropriate for you to share portions with anyone else.

EATING PATTERNS:
- ❏ Only eat when hungry
- ❏ Eat to a schedule
- ❏ Eat sit down meals
- ❏ Eat on the fly
- ❏ Eat balanced meals
- ❏ Eat snack food
- ❏ Binge
- ❏ Binge & purge
- ❏ Eat for comfort whether or not hungry

SLEEP:
- ❏ Am I able to go to sleep easily?
- ❏ Do I wake up much at night?
- ❏ I've had a change in sleeping patterns
- ❏ It's hard to get out of bed

TEARS:
- ❏ Is it easy or hard to cry?
- ❏ When I start crying, I can't stop
- ❏ Crying gives me relief
- ❏ I can cry in front of others
- ❏ I can't cry in front of others
- ❏ I can cry only with someone I know well
- ❏ I burst out crying sometimes
- ❏ I'm embarrassed when I cry
- ❏ I never know when I'll cry

WEIGHT:
- ____ How much do I weigh?
- ____ How much did I weigh a year ago?
- ____ How much did I weigh 5 years ago?
- ____ What is my ideal weight?
- ____ Am I gaining or losing weight?
- ____ Do I want that to happen?

ANGER:
- ❏ I never show my anger
- ❏ I can't contain my anger
- ❏ My anger spills over to others
- ❏ This bothers me or I'm okay with it
- ❏ When I'm angry, I let it out
- ❏ How do I let my anger out?
- ❏ I bear grudges and it's hard to forgive

GUILT:
- ❏ I feel guilty about_____
- ❏ I can talk freely about these feelings
- ❏ I've never told anyone these feelings
- ❏ I experience remorse at times
- ❏ I find talking about my feelings helps

**SPIRITUALLY:**

I feel this way about my spiritual nature:

- ❏ Content
- ❏ Disturbed
- ❏ neutral

❏ My spirituality and my religion are merged
❏ My spirituality and religion are separate for me
❏ I am at peace with myself
❏ I am in inner turmoil about my relationship with the universe

**ANXIETY / PANIC:**

I get panic attacks:

- ❏ Often
- ❏ Occasionally
- ❏ Never

They last for:

- ❏ Days
- ❏ Hours
- ❏ Just moments
- ❏ I can get them under control
- ❏ They are uncontrollable

**SEXUAL FEELINGS:**

I have sexual feelings:

- ❏ Often
- ❏ Sometimes
- ❏ never have any sexual feelings

When I have such feelings

- ❏ I've gone with them
- ❏ repressed them
- ❏ I miss my sexual activity to what degree_____?

**SHARING:**

- ❏ I am aware of those parts of myself I am willing to share, and why
- ❏ I am aware of those parts of myself I am not willing to share, and why

**DREAMS:**

I dream:

- ❏ frequently
- ❏ Occasionally
- ❏ Never

I remember my dreams :

- ❏ Always
- ❏ Sometimes
- ❏ Never

My dreams are mostly:

- ❏ pleasant
- ❏ unpleasant
- ❏ nightmares
- ❏ nightmares with physical effects
- ❏ I keep having the same dream

**FEARS:**

My greatest fear right now is _____ _____ _____.

**CALM SCENE:**

When I am calm, my visualization is _____ _____ _____ _____.

# What does the Bible say?

God heals the brokenhearted and binds up their wounds.

PSALM 147:3

**SUGGESTED SCRIPTURES**

☐ PROVERBS 2:2-5

☐ 2 CORINTHIANS 1:3-11

☐ MATTHEW 5:2-4

As our creator, God knows our hearts and always knows best how to help us. All the answers to life's questions are in the Bible.

When we are grief-stricken, when we talk to God and read his word, we are comforted. Prayer and Bible study are two powerful healing modalities God has offered to help sustain us in both good times and bad. Scriptures provide nourishment for our heart and soul. Whether you feast on the Bible for food and prayer as a snack, allow both to nourish and sustain you when you're hungry for comfort and understanding.

BIBLE ASSIGNMENT 4

## What does the Bible say about understanding and comfort?

**Do you feel the Bible understands your loss? If so, what scriptures do you find helpful? Be prepared to discuss your answers at the next meeting.**

MY SCRIPTURES

ANSWER:

iCARE™ GRIEF MINISTRY GUIDE

# Caring plan

RESILIENCE RX™ TIP 4
## Chromotherapy

Colors are all around us, and they aren't meaningless. They play a role in how we feel, and can influence our emotions and how we react.

Chromotherapy is an ancient practice, yet researchers are just beginning to understand how it works as a healing modality as they study how colors affect our brain and emotions.

There is not one blade of grass, there is no color in this world that is not intended to make us rejoice. JOHN CALVIN

### WHY IT MATTERS

What we know about chromotherapy is that it calms the amygdala, the fear center of the brain. It also takes you outside the thinking part of your brain. Certain colors can invigorate a depressed mood or soothe an agitated mind, lower blood pressure, and relax breathing.

> **SELF CARE**
>
> When you need to relax, grab a coloring book or color the following pages. Use crayons, colored pencils, gel pens or felt pens to color each picture using whatever colors match your emotions in that moment.

### BENEFITS OF ADULT COLORING

Most of us loved coloring as a child. Its popularity as an activity for grownups has exploded, and for good reason. The repetitive hand motions used in coloring induces a meditative state. Focusing on the simple act of coloring gives our brain a respite from pain. It unplugs it from negativity and plugs it into positivity by focusing on the present rather than our worries. The beauty of coloring is that it can be done by anyone regardless of creative talent, and you can take it with you wherever you go. Pick colors that reflect your current mood to help safely externalize your feelings.

### MORE WAYS TO USE COLOR TO TRIGGER POSITIVE HORMONES:

- Paint a color-by-number picture
- Color your bath water
- Plug in a colored nightlight
- Hang a colored glass prism
- Paint the walls of your bedroom or office
- Add colorful home décor
- Use colored bulbs in your lamps
- Enjoy a color wash YouTube video
- Download a color therapy app
- Enjoy a chromotherapy sauna

# CHAPTER 5

## ANGER

**Anger is a natural emotion that needs to be expressed.** When we get angry, a cortisol reaction occurs in the brain that causes an increase in our heart rate, blood pressure, respirations and core body temperature. Too much cortisol will decrease the brain's serotonin, a happy hormone. A decrease in serotonin can make you feel anger and pain more easily.

When we physically and emotionally restrain anger, it can be expressed or manifest in inappropriate ways. Sometimes it results in physical discharges into the body or is expressed through erratic behavior. Other times we suppress it until it becomes a lifetime of bitterness.

**It is important to learn how to externalize anger so it can be released and resolved.**

- It is not a sin to be angry; it is a sin against your being to hold repressed anger.
- Learn to release your anger safely and in a manner that is appropriate for you.

1. Do you know when you're angry? What happens to you physically?
    - ☐ Face turns red
    - ☐ Blood pressure goes up
    - ☐ Tight muscles
    - ☐ Clenched fists
    - ☐ Heart races

2. What happens to you emotionally?
    - ☐ Cry
    - ☐ Yell
    - ☐ Scream
    - ☐ Curse
    - ☐ Feel sad
    - ☐ Feel fear

3. What happens to you spiritually?
    - ☐ Feel guilt
    - ☐ Feel shame

4. As a child, what happened when you displayed your natural anger?

5. Do you feel mad now? If so, what are you mad at? Anger doesn't need to be reasonable or rational. You may be angry at:
    - Medical establishment, individuals or institutions, hospice, etc.
    - The person who died for leaving, not leaving soon enough, drain on finances, for beneficiaries in will, not listening to me about smoking, drinking, etc.
    - Relatives and friends for not visiting, insensitivity, not behaving to my expectations.
    - God for not minding the store, deserting me in hour of need, ignoring my prayers, letting my loved one suffer.
    - Others for murdering my loved one, or for letting him or her abuse oneself.
    - Myself. Anger directed inward is one form of guilt.

6. Discuss how to form a plan to uncover and deal with your anger.

## HIDDEN ANGER

Anger is a natural human emotion. We are all born with the capability of letting others know we are distressed. As infants, we show natural anger by getting red in the face and crying at the top of our lungs. As toddlers, we threw ourselves down and screamed and kicked when we felt angry. Parents scolded or spanked us for doing this, and little by little we learned not to physically express our natural anger or act in a violent fashion.

Perhaps we learned to use words to express anger, such as profanity, sarcastic remarks and vindictive thoughts. Many of us were taught that, too, wasn't nice.

As we matured and grew into nice, polite, civil, socially responsible people, we became quite adept at hiding and repressing our natural anger, so much so that we often convince ourselves we aren't really angry, when deep down our insides might be raging.

Denial and self-deception are ways we learned to tell ourselves we're okay, even though the anger was still there, no matter how well we covered it up.

Would you call yourself an angry person? What do you do with your natural anger? Do you deny negative feelings or just don't get angry?

## ACTIVITY: ANGER SIGNS

Mark the signs of hidden anger which apply to you. Be honest with yourself.

- ❏ Procrastination in the completion of imposed tasks.
- ❏ Perceptual or habitual lateness.
- ❏ A liking for sadistic or ironic humor.
- ❏ Sarcasm, cynicism or flippancy in conversation.
- ❏ Over-politeness, constant cheerfulness, attitude of grin and bear it.
- ❏ Frequent sighing.
- ❏ Smiling while hurting.
- ❏ Frequent disturbing or frightening dreams.
- ❏ Overcontrolled, monotone speaking voice.
- ❏ Difficulty in getting to sleep or sleeping through the night.
- ❏ Boredom, apathy, loss of interest and enthusiasm.
- ❏ Slowing down of movement.
- ❏ Getting tired more easily than usual.
- ❏ Excessive irritability over trifles.
- ❏ Getting drowsy at inappropriate times.
- ❏ Sleeping more than usual, maybe 12 to 14 hours a day.
- ❏ Waking up tired rather than rested and refreshed.
- ❏ Clenched jaws and/or grinding teeth, especially while sleeping.
- ❏ Facial tics, spasmodic foot movements, fist clenching and similar repeated physical acts done unintentionally or unawares.
- ❏ Chronic depression and/or extended periods of feeling down for no reason.
- ❏ Chronically stiff or sore neck.
- ❏ Stomach ulcers.

Don't be surprised if you marked more than a few. Majority of nice adults are going around with hidden anger. Some of us have learned how to discharge our anger in appropriate ways. Some of us have gotten—or will get—physically ill as our body tries to discharge the suppressed anger.

# HOW TO SAFELY PROCESS ANGER

The only way to escape from anger is by confronting it, listening to it, and working it through, just like grief. As a powerful emotion, some are frightened by it, or have been taught to avoid pain. Find ways that allow you to safely process and discharge the anger. Below are some examples to get you started.

### PHYSICAL EXTERNALIZATION

Do something physical that doesn't make you more frustrated (don't continue hitting golf balls if you keep missing them).

- Hit the ground using a rubber hose.
- Beat on pillows.
- Throw a bowling ball.
- Hit golf balls at the driving range.
- Run.
- Chop wood.
- Pound nails.
- Stomp on bubble wrap.

### ACTIVE FORGIVENESS

It's difficult to get on with your life without forgiving those who anger you. This is why externalizing anger is very important, otherwise it's just words without action. Active forgiving involves letting issues pass through, noticing them, and letting them go. The confessional works for some, prayer and personal confession work for others.

### EMOTIONAL EXTERNALIZATION

Do something that allows you to express your frustration and anger.

- Cry, yell and scream.
- Throw a tantrum in your bedroom (this combines physical and emotional release).
- Allow yourself to gut cry.

### INTELLECTUAL EXTERNALIZATION

- Keep a journal and write down how your anger started and how you feel about it. Does it scare you? What do you do about it? Where does it cause you to choke up?
- If you're angry at an individual, write a letter and let it all hang out, and then burn it. If your writing skills need development, take a writing workshop.
- Give yourself permission to talk about your anger in your support group.

### SPIRITUAL EXTERNALIZATION

- Give it to God. Talk to him.
- Spend time in still meditation or listen to spiritually soothing music.
- If your spirituality is closely aligned to your faith or religion, revisit your association with the faith of your youth or the faith of your rebirth.

# What does the Bible say?

For his anger lasts only a moment, but his favor lasts a lifetime; weeping may stay the night but rejoicing comes in the morning.

PSALM 30:5

**SUGGESTED SCRIPTURES**

- 2 SAMUEL 18:33 19:4
- JAMES 1:18-20
- 1 PETER 5:6-10

Anger is a natural human response to pain. The death of someone we love causes severe pain and much suffering of body, mind and spirit. Healing is not easy. The Bible teaches that healing comes from God. We mend best when we leave anger and find understanding and forgiveness through our faith.

Pain may never stop, but how we manage that pain is what will end our suffering. When we turn to God for our strength, we find a new self. Even through pain and suffering, joy and life are obtainable in Christ.

BIBLE ASSIGNMENT 5

## What does the bible say about suffering and anger?

**Do you feel angry that your loved one died? If so, what scriptures do you find helpful? Be prepared to discuss your answers at the next meeting.**

**MY SCRIPTURES**

ANSWER:

iCARE™ GRIEF MINISTRY GUIDE

## Caring Plan

RESILIENCE RX™ TIP 5

### Green Therapy

The 23rd Psalms reminds us that "He makes me lie down in green pastures. He leads me beside the still waters. He restores my soul." Known as green therapy, a stroll of any length through nature offers one of the most reliable boosts to your mental and physical well-being.

There are moments when all anxiety and stated toil are becalmed in the infinite leisure and repose of nature.
HENRY DAVID THOREAU

#### WHY IT MATTERS

Exposing your brain to restorative environments by immersing yourself in the atmosphere of the forest helps with mental fatigue by eliciting feelings of awe. This triggers the brain to release feel-good hormones that counteract the stress hormones of grief.

#### NATURAL THERAPY

Stress, anxiety, and depression may all be eased by some time in the great outdoors, especially when combined with exercise. The natural environment is restorative, and one thing that a walk outside can restore is your waning attention. Doses of nature have found to improve concentration after just 20 minutes in a park. Studies show that walks in the forest were specifically associated with decreased levels of anxiety and bad moods. The effects of nearby water such as a stream, waterfall or fountain improves it even more.

> **SELF CARE**
>
> Try to spend at least twenty minutes outside every day. Even a walk around the block can help. During inclement weather, eat your breakfast or lunch near a window, look at forest images, or watch nature videos on YouTube.

#### WAYS TO ENJOY OUTSIDE

- ☐ Walk, run, bike ride or hike
- ☐ Garden
- ☐ Kayak, sailing or fishing
- ☐ Read a book in a park
- ☐ Golf, play tennis, or swim
- ☐ Recreational sports such as soccer
- ☐ Kite flying
- ☐ Geo-caching
- ☐ Outdoor yoga
- ☐ Metal detecting
- ☐ Mining for gems
- ☐ Outdoor photography

# CHAPTER 6

## GUILT

In the last chapter we mentioned that guilt is often a result of being angry with ourselves. However, that's only part of it.

1. What is guilt?
    - If you had to put guilt in your body, where would it be?
    - If you gave guilt a color, what color would it be?
    - If guilt had a sound, how would it sound?

2. What is your first remembrance of feeling guilty?
    - What were the circumstances surrounding it?
    - Who labeled it for you and told you it was guilt?

3. What productive thing does guilt do for you? Is this thing really productive?

4. Does knowing you are not alone in your guilt help in any way?

5. Who do we need forgiveness from in order to get over the intensity of our feeling? How do we sand down the rough edges?

6. If we need forgiveness from our dead loved one, how are we going to go about getting it?

7. What has to happen to be free from our feelings of guilt?

### ACTIVITY

**Substitute the word guilt for resentment and see what happens.**

I feel **guilty** about not taking good enough care of _____.

I **resent** the demands placed upon me when I was taking care of _____.

# GUILT

Even though we intellectually know we can't undo the past, our inner self will sometimes not let us off the hook. For many of us, the perceived deeds or omissions of the past keep coming back, again and again and again, as if a needle were stuck in an old record. Over and over it keeps whispering . . .

- you should have . . .
- you shouldn't have . . .
- If only you had . . .

Sometimes it is an incessant inside voice which will just not stop, even at 3 in the morning. Sometimes we know our fault is imagined. Though it is not visible to the rest of the world, we still cannot seem to let go.

Sometimes our fault is real—we really were clearly wrong. If we only had a chance to do it over, we would now want to do something quite different.

The uncomfortable feelings we have are known as **guilt**.

- Does it help us to know that guilt is common?
- Does it help to know that in most cases, we couldn't or wouldn't really do anything different if we had another chance, particularly if we were operating with the same information we had at the time?
- Does it help to know we are already forgiven by God?
- Our problem may be that we never really learned how to forgive ourselves.

## HOW THEN, DO WE DEAL WITH GUILT?

Acknowledge its presence by verbalizing it first to ourselves, and then to another person. Make it a clear statement:

- "When Fred was dying, I was cranky and irritable and never really told him I loved him."
- "Would Joan have died by suicide if she hadn't discovered me having an affair?"
- "I knew Joseph's smoking was killing him, and I never successfully got him to stop."
- "I should have stayed at the hospital the night Harvey died. I was tired, and didn't listen to myself. He died alone and I'm so unhappy that we never got to say goodbye."

We may need to express it in many ways, perhaps in writing or in conversation. We may need to act it out. We may need to identify a color, sound or picture to it. A hidden guilt seems to stay with us forever. A guilt that's brought out into the open loses its power to haunt us.

## HOW DO WE DEAL WITH OTHERS?

Some people want to tell us that our guilt is groundless, that we couldn't have acted any other way and shouldn't feel the way we do. While most of these comments are gratuitous, at some level it may be helpful to hear that the rest of the world doesn't appear to judge us as harshly as we are judging ourselves. We sometimes have a difficult time listening to these well-meaning people because we know they are incapable of really knowing what we are feeling.

## CLARITY

Our feelings are justified in our eyes at the moment we are feeling the way we do. What we often don't recognize is that our perspective is frequently obscured by the traumatic events which have taken place. As we gain clarity, our perspective changes. Our feelings of guilt also have the ability to change.

### How do we go about gaining clarity?

Once acknowledging our guilty feelings and listening to others tell us why we should or shouldn't feel this way, it is helpful to clearly review the circumstances which led to our feelings. These should be written down to ensure we haven't missed anything. The next step is to list all the reasons we might be feeling and reacting the way we are. Also list the mitigating circumstances which help to explain why we acted that way.

## RESENTMENT

Many psychologists have found a link between resentment and guilt. Since guilt is often a reaction to things resented, it is sometimes useful for us to list all the people, circumstances or things we resented which feeds our guilt.

Examples:
- I resent having had the responsibility to decide whether Henry remained on life support.
- I resent that I was put in the position of needing to be Harry's nurse for the last 3 years. I never asked for that role nor was I particularly qualified for it.
- I resent that Joan treated me so poorly that I felt I needed other personal companionship.
- I resent that I wasn't able to say goodbye.

## EXERCISE

For each guilt, put the words **I resent** before the situation. Does it talk to you? Can you associate with the resentment within the situation which you are now using to abuse yourself?

## What does the Bible say?

Happy is the person whom the Lord does not consider guilty, and in whom there is nothing false.

PSALM 32:1-5

**SUGGESTED SCRIPTURES**

- PROVERBS 14:10-18
- EPHESIANS 4:29-32
- HEBREWS 12:14-15

Guilt and resentment are normal emotions that are quite common after loss. Those who experience guilt often feel as though they are somehow responsible for the death of their loved one. Those who experience resentment may feel as though someone else was responsible for your suffering.

If not addressed, guilt and resentment wear us down into someone we don't want to be. It also holds no power over the person you're angry at, only you. The only way through is to first be aware that you harbor guilt and/or resentment, and then make the decision to work on releasing it. As you do, give yourself grace, and trust that God knows you did the best you could at the time. Ask Him to help you release your guilt and resentment.

Another step is to make the conscious choice to develop gratitude—thanking God for what we do have. When you do, the power of resentment and guilt fade.

BIBLE ASSIGNMENT 6

## What does the Bible say about guilt and resentment?

**Do you feel guilt or resentment about your loss? If so, what scriptures do you find helpful? Be prepared to discuss your answers at the next meeting.**

ANSWER:

MY SCRIPTURES

# Caring Plan

RESILIENCE RX™ TIP 6

## Dance/Movement Therapy

Feelings can influence your movement, and movement can impact your feelings. When we feel tired and sad, we tend to move more slowly. Moving your body improves your mood, helps combat anxiety and depression, and promotes a safe space for the expression of feeling.

When you dance, your purpose is not to get to a certain place on the floor. It's to enjoy each step along the way.

DR. WAYNE DYER

### WHY IT WORKS

Any form of exercise is great for relieving stress in the mind and body. Dancing is also emotionally therapeutic, especially when paired with music we love. Since movement can be related to thoughts and feelings, dance/movement therapy (DMT) benefits us both physically and mentally through stress reduction, mood management, decreased muscle tension, increased mobility and more. Further, it oxygenates the brain, which helps clear the mind and allows you more clarity and focus.

> **SELF CARE**
>
> Put on music you love, and dance for ten minutes every day like nobody's watching. If you feel inhibited, dance in the shower, your bedroom, or a corner of your garden.

### PHYSICAL BENEFITS

Dancing helps to oxygenate the brain and fight illness. Unlike the circulatory or respiratory systems, the lymphatic system— the body's defense mechanism against illness—does not have a pump. It relies on your motion to circulate the fluid that contains infection-fighting white blood cells around the body. Each time you move large muscles of the body, you help pump lymphatic fluid through your body, keeping your systems circulating.

### TAKE A MENTAL RECESS

School recess was invented for a reason. Movement improves cognitive performance for people of all ages. In one study, children who participated in physical activity demonstrated increased electrical activity in the brain, as well as improved mental accuracy and reaction times during learning. Dancing and moving offer a mental recess through physical release.

Movement is one of the most basic functions of the human body, making it easy to incorporate motion into daily life in a way that feels good. If dancing isn't your thing, try one of the alternatives.

**ALTERNATIVE OPTIONS TO DANCING:**

- Shake a bed sheet.
- Run in place or jump up and down.
- Stretch or roll your head in circles.
- Go for a short walk.
- Squeeze a rubbery stress ball.
- Window shop.
- Garden.
- Stretch.
- Clean a closet.
- Grocery shop with a basket instead of a cart.
- Romp around with the kids or grandkids
- Walk, bike, or hike.

# CHAPTER 7

## RECONCILIATION

We've all heard the cliché "time heals," yet we know that time itself just doesn't make it suddenly all right. We know that from moment to moment we are never quite the same.

The experience of each moment changes our outlook on the next moment. The changing of perspective can work for you, once you realize and accept that the world is never static.

1. What are your feelings?
2. What have you been experiencing?
3. What are you looking forward to experiencing?

### ACTIVITY

Review the steps of reconciliation. Where are you with these?

- ❏ Learn to effectively experience and express the reality of the death of your loved one.
- ❏ Learn to lean into the pain of the loss, while learning how to nurture yourself physically, emotionally and spiritually.
- ❏ Learn to convert your relationship with the person who died from one of interactive presence to one of appropriate memory.
- ❏ Learn to develop a new self-identity based on a life without the person who died.
- ❏ Learn to relate the experience of the death to a context of new meaning in your life.
- ❏ Learn to develop a lasting network of support to help you through the process.

# WHAT I NEED

### TIME

I need time alone, and time with others whom I can trust and will listen when I need to talk. I need time to feel and understand the feelings which go along with loss.

### REST

I may need extra amounts of things I needed before. Relaxation, exercise, diversion, nourishment, hot baths, afternoon naps, a trip, a cause to work for to help others, any of these may give me a lift. Grief is an emotionally exhausting process. I need to replenish myself, to follow what feels healing, and connects me to the people and things I love.

### SECURITY

I need to reduce or find help for financial or other stresses in my life. I need to allow myself to be close to ones I can trust. It helps when I allow myself to return to a routine and to do things at my own pace.

### HOPE

I find hope and comfort from those who have experienced a similar loss. Knowing some things that helped them, and realizing that they have recovered and that time does help, gives me hope that sometime in the future my grief will be less raw and less painful.

### CARING

I try to allow myself to accept the expressions of caring from others, even though they may be uneasy and awkward. Helping a friend or relative also suffering from the same loss often brings me a feeling of closeness with that person.

### SMALL PLEASURE

I no longer underestimate the healing effects of small pleasures. Sunsets, a walk in the woods, a favorite food all are small steps toward regaining pleasure in life.

### GOALS

It can sometimes feel that much of life is without meaning. At times like these, small goals are helpful. Giving myself something to look forward to, like playing tennis with a friend next week, a movie tomorrow night, a trip next month, helps me get through the moment. Living one day at a time is a good rule of thumb. At first, my enjoyment of these things just isn't the same. I know this is normal. As time passes, I will work on longer range goals to give some structure and direction to my life. It is okay to get some guidance or counseling to help with this.

### MEDICATION

Unless carefully managed under professional supervision, medication is not always the answer. Drugs intended to help me get through periods of shock may delay the necessary process of grieving. I cannot prevent or cure grief. The only way **out** is **through**.

### BACKSLIDING

Sometimes after a period of feeling good, I find myself back in extreme sadness. I know the nature of grief is up and down, and it may happen over and over for a time. Humans cannot take in the pain of death all at once. I give myself permission to let it in a little at a time.

# GRIEFWORK & BOUNDARIES

A boundary is a limit or edge that defines you as separate from others. When that boundary is indistinguishable from the boundary of others, the relationship is called **enmeshed**. When someone crosses your boundary without your full consent, your boundary has been **violated**.

An understanding of boundaries, those which have been appropriately healthy for you and your past, current and future relationships, is particularly useful when dealing with the changes brought by the death of someone who has been a significant part of your life.

You might discover that your boundaries were inappropriately enmeshed with a deceased partner, or even violated by that partner. In order to constructively deal with your loss, you may need to better understand that relationship and learn whether or not there is a danger of having it adversely affect your future well-being. Many changes will be brought about by your loss, and a better understanding of your rightful boundaries is an important part of shaping that change in a healthy manner.

While problems in life are inevitable, suffering is not. You are allowed to make appropriate changes in your image, outlook and behavior.

### BOUNDARY TYPES

- **Physical.** A boundary may be physical, like where and when you are comfortable being touched by others, how close you want to be to others, how physically involved you are comfortable being with others. It is in respect for the accidental violation of another's physical boundary that in our first session we asked you not to hug or physically comfort another without first getting that person's consent. We cannot assume that someone else's boundary is the same as our own.

- **Emotional.** A boundary may also be emotional, a result of how you act with others or will permit others to act with you, communicate with you, be with you, and how you permit yourself to feel in a variety of life situations.

- **Visible.** A boundary may be visible, obvious or apparent to you and to others, or invisible, where you or others are not aware that it exists or even that it has been violated.

Given a particular relationship or situation, your boundary may be different than usual. There are appropriate boundaries and inappropriate boundaries for you in varying situations and relationships. Your boundaries were learned as a result of your experiences as children and in the process of growing up. Because you may have learned a set of inappropriate boundaries, this doesn't mean that you can't change your life and learn to practice more appropriate boundaries.

### PHYSICAL BOUNDARIES

You have a right to have control of your body. You need not let anyone get closer to you than what is comfortable for you. Sometimes we're conditioned to accept something as outwardly comfortable which, had we been in good communication with our inside feelings, would have realized was making us uncomfortable. Incidentally, this is true for emotional as well as physical boundaries. Insist that your boundary of physical closeness, sexual contact, and degree of touch are honored and not **violated**.

### EMOTIONAL BOUNDARIES

Emotional boundaries are more varied, more invisible, more deeply ingrained in your upbringing, and sometimes more difficult to change.

# What does the Bible say?

Everyone needs times to laugh and dance, but we also need times to weep and mourn.

ECCLESIASTES 3:4

**SUGGESTED SCRIPTURES**

- PHILIPPIANS 3:13-14
- PHILIPPIANS 4:7-9
- ROMANS 8:12-21

Spiritual growth takes place more in difficult times than easy times. When a loved one dies, it's a valuable time to reflect on your own mortality and your relationship with God.

It has been said, "An open casket can be worth a thousand sermons." Some people avoid funerals and visiting people in hospitals and nursing homes because these situations make them feel uncomfortable. But to be a healer, you must go where people are hurting. If you do, your unselfishness will help you grow.

BIBLE ASSIGNMENT 7

## What spiritual lessons can we learn from loss and grief?

**Do you believe we can learn from our hardships? If so, what scriptures do you find helpful? Be prepared to discuss your answers at the next meeting.**

MY SCRIPTURES

ANSWER:

iCARE™ GRIEF MINISTRY GUIDE

# Caring Plan

RESILIENCE RX™ TIP 7
## Laugh Therapy

Those who need a good laugh are usually the ones who feel least like laughing, yet the heart can hold joy the same time as sorrow, so go ahead and laugh. One laugh can scatter a hundred griefs, and help lift your spirits. Even in difficult times, a laugh—or even simply a smile—can go a long way.

Laughter is an instant vacation. MILTON BERLE

### WHY IT MATTERS

Laughter creates the perfect diaphragmatic breath that oxygenates the brain. It also stimulates the brain into a positive state, which helps clear the mind and allows you more clarity and focus. When you're having a tough time, laughing creates psychological distance and can slow the momentum of overwhelm, frustration or disappointment.

A powerful healing modality, studies show that laughter offers many physical, psychological, and emotional benefits. Smiling and laughter stimulate the facial muscles that trigger the brain to release happy hormones called endorphins, the body's natural feel-good chemicals that promote an overall sense of well-being, temporarily relieves pain, decreases stress, and increases immune and infection-fighting antibodies.

> **SELF CARE**
>
> Enjoy a good belly laugh at least once every day to oxygenate the brain and trigger feel-good hormones. Ten minutes of laughter is equivalent to thirty minutes on a cardio machine.

### BENEFITS OF LAUGH THERAPY

Because the body can't tell the difference between a real or fake smile, hold a pencil between your teeth to "fake it until you make it." When you smile, the stimulation of the involved facial muscles trigger the brain to release the chemicals that cause the feeling of happiness. A phenomenon called facial feedback, this works even if you weren't feeling happy in the first place. The brain can't tell the difference and will be tricked into releasing those feel-good chemicals anyway.

No matter how you choose to induce a good belly laugh, the bottom line is that whatever makes you laugh is truly good medicine.

## WHY IT WORKS:

- Laughter and crying are like yin and yang, they both release energy.
- Laughing bypasses the mind and helps us keep a positive attitude.
- Laughter engages in perfect diaphragmatic breath. When we laugh, we exhale completely and then inhale completely, which oxygenates the brain and body. When our brains are fully oxygenated, our minds become calm and clear.
- Laughter releases endorphins which help us feel good. The brain oxygenation and endorphins combination are like a Joyful cocktail.
- When we feel good and the mind is clear, we feel grounded and peaceful, less stress and less reactive.
- Laughter doesn't change reality but does help us to cultivate a positive mental attitude.
- Be silly, be playful. Laughter is contagious and allows our inner child to come out.
- Fake laughter often turns into authentic laughter. The body can't tell the difference, and the health benefits are the same.

## HOW TO LAUGH WHEN YOU DON'T FEEL LIKE IT:

- Watch a comedy movie or TV show
- Watch funny YouTube videos
- Listen to children laughing
- Watch blooper reels on TV
- Read a funny book
- Try laugh yoga
- Look at funny pictures
- Read funny social media memes
- Listen to funny jokes

**Not every day is beautiful,
but there is beauty in ever day.**

LYNDA CHELDELIN FELL

# SESSION 8

## TURNING PAIN INTO PURPOSE

In this final chapter, we encourage you to explore how you can turn pain into purpose either by helping others who are grieving, too, or finding a new purpose in life.

- ❏ How do you view your life now?
- ❏ What meaning have you found, and how can you use that new meaning to create joy?

## GIVE JOY

Winston Churchill once said, "We make a living by what we get. We make a life by what we give." In other words, helping others helps our own heart to heal.

Giving is good for the giver in that it induces a natural high. It generates positive emotions that trigger a release of dopamine which regulates pleasure in the brain. It also evokes internal gratitude which helps to heal our heart.

Additional bonuses are the multiple—and proven—health benefits of giving: less stress, lower blood pressure, improved sleep, increased self-esteem, and greater happiness.

### WAYS TO GIVE:

- Distribute blessing bags to the homeless.
- Volunteer in the community.
- Donate to a charity.
- Smile at a stranger.
- Give a compliment.
- Leave a nice note for someone at work or school.
- Let a driver merge in front of you during rush hour traffic.
- Do random acts of kindness.
- Feed the homeless in a soup kitchen.
- Hold the door open for someone behind you.
- Send an anonymous care package to someone who is struggling.

**She who heals others heals herself.**

LYNDA CHELDELIN FELL

# TURNING PAIN INTO PURPOSE

When I was a kid, I wanted to be a doctor. A brain surgeon. But God has a way of throwing us curve balls that force us down a different path.

Sometimes those paths are most welcome, like mothering four wonderful children. My least favorite? Losing a child. That path is long and torturous, and took me straight through the belly of hell.

My story began one night in 2007, when I had a vivid dream. I was the front passenger in a car and my daughter Aly was sitting behind the driver. Suddenly the car missed a curve and sailed into a lake. The driver and I escaped the sinking car, but Aly did not.

My beloved daughter was gone. The only thing she left behind was a book floating in the water where she disappeared.

Two years later, in August 2009, that horrible nightmare came true when Aly died as a back seat passenger in a car accident.

Returning home from a swim meet, the car carrying Aly was T-boned by a father coming home from work. My beautiful fifteen-year-old daughter took the brunt of the impact and died instantly. She was the only fatality.

**Life couldn't get any worse, right? Wrong. Hell wasn't done with me yet.**

My dear hubby buried his grief in the sand. He escaped into 80-hour work weeks, more wine, more food, and less talking. His blood pressure shot up, his cholesterol went off the chart, and the perfect storm arrived on June 4, 2012. My husband suddenly began drooling and couldn't speak. At age 46, my soulmate was having a major stroke.

My dear hubby lived, but he couldn't talk, read, or write, and his right side was paralyzed. He needed help just to sit up in bed. He needed full-time care.

Still reeling from the loss of our daughter, I found myself again thrust into a fog of grief so thick, I couldn't see through the storm. Autopilot resumed its familiar place at the helm.

I needed God's reassurance that the sun was on the other side of hell. As I fought my way through the storm, He showed me that helping others was a powerful way to heal my own heart. I began reaching out to individuals who were adrift and in need of a warm hug.

In 2013, I formed AlyBlue Media to house my mission. Comforting people who spoke my language and listening to their stories, my mission took on a life of its own and came in many forms: a radio show, film, webinars, and writing. I also hosted a national convention. I wanted to bring the broken-hearted together.

I had many wonderful speakers, but the one who excited me most was a woman who had faced seven losses in a few short years—Martin Luther King's youngest daughter.

I didn't bring Dr. Bernice King to the convention to tell us about her famous father—we already knew that story. I wanted to know how she survived.

Over the course of that weekend, I was deeply moved by watching strangers swap stories and become newfound friends. These were stories born from hardship and yet remarkable on many levels.

**Touched to the core, I set out to capture them into a book series aptly named Grief Diaries.**

Now home to 5 literary awards and more than 700 writers spanning the globe, Grief Diaries has over 35 titles in print. Two years later I founded the International Grief Institute to help others invest in community resilience and strengthen the pipeline of hope.

I wanted to be a brain surgeon, but God had other plans. Being thrown into the forge so He could mold my soul was necessary for Him to accomplish those plans.

Life's lessons aren't easy because as humans, we don't learn from the easy stuff. It's some-times necessary to reduce us like molten metal before we can be forged into a pillar of hope, courage, strength—or whatever God wants us to be—so we can serve others.

Once the forging was done, He filled my life—and heart—with blessings for which I am truly grateful, blessings that wouldn't have come about any other way. He'll do the same for you.

**Where am I today?**

Once a bereaved mother, always a bereaved mother. My heart is a bit like a broken teacup that's been glued back together. All the pieces are there, but they might not fit as seamlessly as they once did.

Some days the glue is strong and unyielding. Other days that glue is soft and threatens to spring a leak. Nonetheless, that teacup still holds water and serves God's purpose.

It's important to hold out hope that the sun can be found at the end of the path. But until you find it, it's comforting to know you aren't alone. God is there, even when you don't think He is.

For the record, I've found the sun. Some days I marvel at its beauty. Other days it hides behind clouds. But I now know those days don't last forever. And thanks to the lessons I've learned from my loss and trusting God along the way, my umbrella is stronger than ever.

Long story short, if I can turn pain into purpose, you can, too. Maybe not right this minute, but when God feels you're ready, he'll point you in the right direction.

Just trust that there is a bigger picture at play, and remember that He's not asking you to save the world, just help one person at a time.

In doing so, you'll help your own heart to heal.

LYNDA CHELDELIN FELL

# FROM DESPAIR TO HOPE

On September 1, 1989, I lost my baby. She died two hours and nine minutes after birth. We named her Aubrie Marie.

During my pregnancy we'd been told that there might be a problem, but everything could be fixed. Although we anticipated a crisis, never did we expect our baby to die.

The year prior, in December 1988, my mother died from a sudden heart attack. She was just fifty-three years old. Six months later I lost a dear friend who had been a mother figure to me. I was no stranger to loss, even then.

My grandmother, who raised me, died when I was fifteen following complications of surgery for brain cancer.

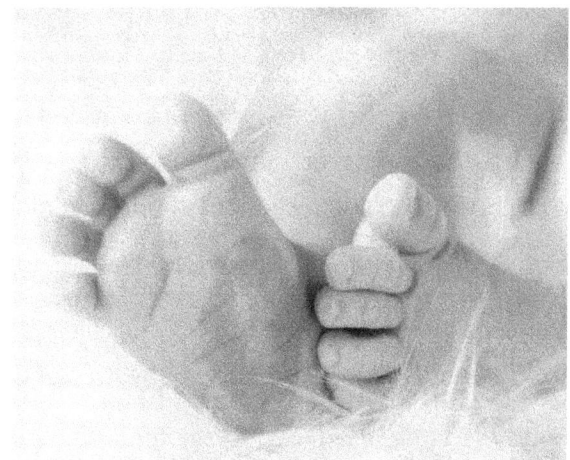

When my baby died, I had no idea where I was to go from there.

After five long days in the hospital, I remember waiting in the doorway for my husband to pull the car around. I wondered, how do I step foot outside without my baby in my arms?

The pain and sorrow were excruciating.

I spent five days physically recuperating from the cesarean section. It happened to be Labor Day weekend that year. The hospital staff was scarce. We were left pretty much alone to deal with our loss.

We weren't told much. As a matter of fact, we weren't even told what the sex of our baby was. We didn't find out that our baby was a girl until my discharge, when a vital statistics lady came to my room to ask why we hadn't checked the box indicating the sex of the baby on the birth certificate form.

She couldn't believe nobody had told us whether our baby was a boy or girl.

She left our room, went down to the morgue to speak with the pathologist who performed the autopsy, and returned twenty minutes later to tell us that we had had a baby girl.

During the five days that followed the birth and death of our baby, we were told the following:

- You are young, you can have another baby.
- God must have wanted an angel in heaven.
- These things are meant to be.
- Why do you have to name it?
- God wanted a grandchild to give to your mother in heaven.
- You should get pregnant right away.
- This usually happens to boy babies.
- You have to call a funeral home.
- These things are meant to be.

Overcome with shock, I couldn't imagine why we had to call a funeral home. Some of these things were told to us by well-meaning friends and family. We were devastated, in shock.

There were no answers, only lots of painful questions coupled with confusion and great sorrow.

The following months were terrible. I didn't have the support I needed. But not because nobody cared—it was because nobody under-stood.

Because of my loss and the short life of my first baby, Aubrie Marie, it has become my life mission to provide that understanding and support to other people who are grieving. As a result, I founded Mourning Discoveries Grief Support Services.

**I wanted to provide a place where people can receive the support and understanding they need following death of a loved one.**

I've since partnered with over three hundred funeral firms in twenty-five states and Canada, and have mailed thousands of publications to grieving families. I have talked to thousands of grieving individuals, and spent countless hours listening to their stories of loss.

Mourning Discoveries is now part of the Inter-national Grief Institute.

We continue to have the honor of providing bereavement support services, facilitate grief support groups, and make a difference in the lives of those who walk the road of grief.

**Because of my own loss, I've helped many navigate through grief towards healing.**

Most importantly, I have been a witness to the power of God's love and the miracle of healing and human resilience.

If it hadn't been for the loss of my precious baby, Aubrie Marie, none of this would've been possible.

I am grateful.

LINDA FINDLAY

# WHAT NOW?

So, you've almost completed a grief ministry training. What were your expectations?

Some entered this experience with hopes that something would happen which would make the pain go all away. Others suspected that the grief ministry would not be a magic pill, yet it might help. Some had no defined expectations, just knew inside that they needed to do something, and this was here to do.

Early on, we learned that this is griefwork, with an emphasis on **work**. Take a measurement of where you are in the reconciliation process. This may help to focus your energies as you continue your work within and outside the church.

- We learned to effectively experience and express outside ourselves the reality of the death. For many, this class was the first opportunity to do this. For others, it was a continuation and reinforcement of what was started elsewhere. It is necessary to continue the process of outside expression of our feelings, whether that be talking regularly to others, writing in our journals, or any other form of outside expression.

- We have learned to allow ourselves to embrace the pain of the loss while learning how to nurture ourselves physically, emotionally and spiritually. Over and over we heard that the only way **out** is **through**. When I am in a safe place, I will permit my feelings to surface and be experienced. Stifling the pain prolongs the agony. This is also a time for learning or relearning how to care for our physical, emotional, and spiritual selves.

- We are learning how to convert our relationship with the person who died from an interactive presence to one of appropriate memory. This is a process which can't be deliberately willed. We have learned to just make a mental note of it as something which is in the process of happening at a subconscious level, and to allow our subconscious to do its work without interference.

- We are learning how to develop a new self-identity based on a life without the person who died. Each person's journey is different, and our individual timing is unique. Each day, some experience takes place which continues to build our new self-identity. For some who had a deeply enmeshed relationship, this may be a difficult task. It isn't a sign of weakness to seek professional help.

- We've begun to relate the experience of the death to a context of new meaning in our lives. For many, death provokes questions regarding the meaning of life and its transitory nature. There are no universal answers to many of these questions, however the process of seeking them often brings a meaningful answer to each of us. I will allow myself time for my own discovery of meaning. I won't permit others to rush me with their pat conclusions.

- I am developing a lasting network of support to help me through the process. This class was a useful step toward learning to establish lasting support. Through our emphasis on social networking, it reinforced my ability to reach out. Sometimes this was easy, other times it wasn't. I will keep trying because I know that continuing to reach out will help my reconciliation timetable. I will find it also causes other miracles in the world. I will try to notice them when they occur.

- Tell others clearly what you want and need for the holidays. Do not be embarrassed or shy to let others know what you want from them in terms of emotional support, help, or sharing. Mindreading is best left to fortunetellers. Unknown expectations generally go unfulfilled and lead to disappointment and bad feelings.

- Honor the old, create the new. If this is the first holiday without your family member, include your deceased loved one to the extent that you can. The memory of him or her will be with you this holiday season no matter what you do. Consider giving gifts in acknowledgment of your dying family member or in memory of the deceased; consider giving love to others in honor of the love you have received. Only you can put the joy into the holidays.

- Be generous to yourself. The holidays are a time of real and symbolic gift-giving. What are you giving yourself this season? When the new year rolls in, what will be your answer to the question, "What supportive and caring thing did I do for myself this holiday season?"

- Celebrate life. It seems like an impossibility for someone in grief to find joy and peace at any time, but especially during the season for joy and peace. This is your challenge. Life is worth living only to the extent that we make it so. Survivorship means more than merely surviving; it means fully living. Search for the living path for you and start now!

This material was prepared by Ellen S. Zinner, Psy.D., and based on materials developed in part by Sally Featherstone, RN.

# GOD'S SCRIPT

On the night of the accident, I sat next to my daughter's body at the scene of the two-car collision. As I sought to find her hand under the white sheet, God handed me a new script. I handed it back.

I wanted my old life, not a new one.

I wanted my daughter to open her eyes, to say "Hi, Mom."

Surveying the car's damage, instinctively I knew that wasn't going to happen. Yet shock, and the horror of seeing my daughter's bare toes peeking out from under the white sheet protected my mind from reality.

**God again handed me the new script. I tore it up and handed it back.**

"I don't want your new script!" I yelled.

I had a wonderful life as a mother of one college graduate, one college student, and two teenagers. My husband and I were even blessed with our first grandchild. Life was wonderful! There was no need for God to go changing it.

But I didn't win. God did. I had no choice but to take the new script.

I ignored it for three years. And then tragedy struck again.

My dear hubby's grief consumed him, and he suffered a life-threatening stroke that left him disabled. He was just 46 years old.

I gave in and waved the white flag. There was nothing left of me. I was done. Exhausted. Here I was facing a new kind of grief, and I had hardly begun to process the first.

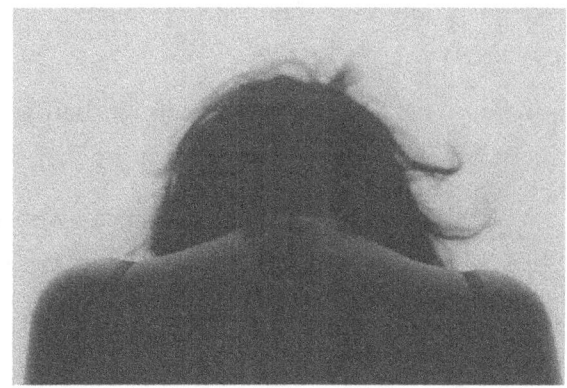

God's script laid there for months and months. My heart broken in so many places, I had no energy to read it. The lines blurred together, the words indistinguishable.

**And then one day out of anger, I picked it up.**

The first line said, "When you help others, you help your own heart to heal."

Seriously, God? I felt like a regressed teenager challenging a parent. I could hardly put one foot in front of the other, how was I supposed to help someone else? But God didn't include instructions. I wasn't amused.

And yet I needed God. Desperately.

I gave in and waved the white flag. I was standing squarely in the belly of hell; I had nothing more to lose.

I wasn't entirely sure how to go about this new script, but herein lies the answer: I didn't have to figure it out all on my own.

One door opened, then two doors, then four. And so on and so forth.

It's now been seven years since the loss of our daughter and four years since my husband's life-changing stroke. I haven't figured it all out yet, but God's script gave me a life purpose far better than I could ever have imagined.

Where am I now? Today, I help others. Because this helps my own heart to heal.

**There. I said it. Script accepted. God was right.**

Helping others has come in many forms. One of my most joyous endeavors was creating the book series, Grief Diaries, an anthology of stories about surviving loss.

When I set out to compile these stories, some questioned whether I had lost my final marble. Who would want to read tales of life's most challenging moments? Yet, God had laid this on my heart.

I trusted God's script, and strangers I've never met handed me the most precious of gift of all: their own loss experiences.

They entrusted me to handle each with kid gloves, package them oh-so-carefully, and present them to the world for the sole purpose of helping others not feel so alone. Each stranger became my friend who enriched my world beyond measure.

So, I no longer questioned the script. I just followed it, never once forgetting that every story I now held in the palm of my hand is sacred. Not just to the writer, but to the world.

**And to God.**

Suddenly, this crazy book series about sharing true stories about loss has given a platform to more than 700 writers.

It feels good to share our experiences with others. Why? Because it helps both readers and writers feel less alone.

**So, it's true. When we help others, we help our own heart to heal.**

Baring and sharing to comfort others like ourselves. Healing hearts by sharing journeys.

**Script accepted.**

Thank you, God.

LYNDA CHELDELIN FELL (2016)

## What does the Bible say?

Who comforts us in all our tribulation, that we may be able to comfort those who are in any trouble with the comfort with which we ourselves are comforted by God.

2 CORINTHIANS 1:4

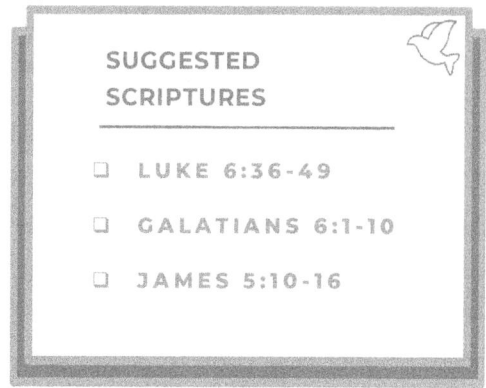

**SUGGESTED SCRIPTURES**

☐ LUKE 6:36-49

☐ GALATIANS 6:1-10

☐ JAMES 5:10-16

Often times, loss and grief lead to deeper compassion. It opens our heart to the needs around us, and we see a clearer picture of the world outside our own.

Giving is good for the giver in that when we help others, it helps our own heart to heal. Find ways to give joy so you, in turn, can receive joy. When you do, as you move forward in your own reconciliation, you give hope to those who are behind you. Allow yourself to be the light so others can see in the dark, just as Christ did for us.

BIBLE ASSIGNMENT 8

### What does the Bible say about helping others who are suffering?

**Has your own loss expanded your compassion toward others? If so, what scriptures do you find helpful? Be prepared to discuss your answers at the next meeting.**

**MY SCRIPTURES**

ANSWER:

## RESILIENCE RX™
## Coping with grief at work

The wealth of a company is built on the health of its employees. When grief impacts our life, the emotional stress and mental exhaustion make us less organized, less productive, and less efficient. Emotional depletion can lead to other health problems such as insomnia, hypertension, and more. Use the tips below manage grief when you return to work. Stay in contact with your boss or human resources to make sure they are supporting you in your time of need.

Self-compassion involves a consistent attitude of kindness and acceptance toward ourselves as a whole.

LISA FIRESTONE, Ph.D.

### SELF CARE TIPS FOR WORK:

- Work with your employer to identify a safe room you can use for 10 to 15 minutes when emotions bubble to the surface. This gives you the space to collect yourself in a private setting away from clients and colleagues.
- Compartmentalize if needed at work but give yourself time to grieve, too.
- If possible, request short-term light cognitive duty to minimize mistakes and injuries.
- Avoid operating dangerous equipment until the fog lifts. This will maximize safety and minimize risk management issues.
- Learn to let go, say no, and ask for help from others. Honor your own limits.

### SELF CARE TIPS FOR HOME:

- Talk about your loss for at least 15 minutes every day. It's okay to ramble, rant, and repeat yourself. Talking is how we process. Processing is how we heal.
- Carve time in your schedule to do things you love. This will help recharge your battery.
- Eat healthy and stay hydrated to boost immunity and physical well-being.
- Engage in light exercise and practice good sleep hygiene.
- Sing. In the shower, in the car, in your bed. It releases muscle tension and stress.
- Enjoy a good belly laugh every day. Laughter releases tension, boosts your mood, and lightens a heavy heart. Watch a comedy or funny videos.
- Engage in activities involving repetitive hand motions such as beading, painting, pottery, knitting, gardening, woodworking or coloring. Repetitive hand motions calms the mind.
- Use journaling to release inner thoughts and feelings.
- Recognize that you can't fix grief. It's a rite of passage for everyone.

# Caring Plan

RESILIENCE RX™ TIP·8

## Hug Therapy

Giving is good for the giver in that a hug benefits ourselves and others. Connections are fostered when people acknowledge and appreciate one another. Hugging is also known to boost self-esteem in people of all ages.

A hug is a free, easy, and—at 20 seconds—a quick way to show love and appreciation.

We need 4 hugs a day for survival, 8 hugs a day for maintenance, 12 hugs a day for growth.   VIRGINIA SATIR

### WHY IT MATTERS

From the time we're born, our family's touch shows us that we're loved and special. The associations of self-worth and tactile sensations from our early years become imbedded in our nervous system as we grow into adults.

A sincere embrace triggers the brain to release the love hormone oxytocin. This substance has many benefits in our physical and mental health. A natural tranquilizer, it helps us to relax, to feel safe and calm our fears and anxiety. And it's free every time we hug, cradle a child, cherish a dog or cat, slow dance, or simply hold the shoulders of a friend.

---

**SELF CARE**

**The average hug between two people is 3 seconds. Research shows that a hug lasting at least 20 seconds has a therapeutic effect on the body and mind. Hug something or something for at least 20 seconds every day.**

---

### BENEFITS OF HUG THERAPY:

Almost 70 percent of communication is nonverbal. Hugging is an excellent method of expressing yourself nonverbally to another human being or animal. Not only can they feel the love and care in your embrace, but they can actually be receptive enough to pay it back.

Hugs stimulate oxytocin, a neurotransmitter that acts on the limbic system, the brain's emotional center. Oxytocin is known to:

- promote contentment
- reduce anxiety and stress
- lower our heart rate
- lower our cortisol level, the hormone responsible for stress
- Released during childbirth, helping mothers forget about the labor they endured and fall immediately in love with their newborn

## HUGS ALSO . . .

Affection also has a direct response on the reduction of stress which prevents many diseases. Touch Research Institute at the University of Miami School of Medicine has carried out more than 100 studies on the power of touch, and discovered evidence of improved immune system, reduced pain, lower glucose levels, and faster growth in premature babies.

- Hugs apply gentle pressure on the sternum which stimulates the thymus gland, which regulates and balances the production of white blood cells, which keep you healthy and disease free.
- Hugs stimulate brains to release dopamine, the pleasure hormone, which helps to negate sadness.
- Hugging also releases serotonin levels, elevating mood and creating happiness.
- Hugs balance out the nervous system. Skin contains a network of tiny pressure centers that can sense touch and notify the brain through the vagus nerve. The galvanic skin response of someone receiving and giving a hug shows a change in skin conductance which suggests a more balanced state in the parasympathetic nervous system.

iCARE™ GRIEF MINISTRY GUIDE

# RESILIENCE RX™
## 10 tips to surviving the holidays

After losing someone you love, the holidays can feel anything but joyful, especially when faced with what to do with our loved one's empty place at the table and Christmas stocking. Allow yourself to try a handful of the suggestions below to guide you through the hustle and bustle, and gift yourself with plenty of compassion, kindness, and grace by doing whatever feels best to your heart.

### TIP #1: MAINTAIN YOUR ROUTINE

A familiar routine offers a sense of reassurance that at least one thing in life hasn't changed, and the familiarity can help ground us through the holiday hustle. But if the idea of sticking to routine is more than you can bear, then honor your need to break tradition. In short, do what feels most soothing to your heart and apologize to no one.

### TIP #2: PROTECT YOUR TIME

Give yourself lots of breathing room and avoid packing the schedule too full. Grieving is emotionally exhausting; plenty of rest will help minimize raw nerves through the flurry of shopping, school performances, and parties.

### TIP #3: CUT YOURSELF SOME SLACK, NOT YOUR FINGER

Cut some slack and buy store-bought. Grieving is naturally distracting, and the ER isn't a great place to dine. Even the smallest kitchen disaster can quickly deplete coping skills. If the family expects your legendary dinner rolls, then cheat with gourmet mashed potatoes and gravy from the deli.

### TRIP #4: SKIP THE CHAOS

Turn off the computer, light a fragrant candle, grab a soft blanket, and binge-watch a good comedy. Take time to create peaceful surroundings to soothe your nerves.

### TIP #5: CRY

Give in to the tears. There is no shortage of raw emotions over the holidays, and crying is not a sign of weakness. It's how we release intense feelings. A good cry can be very healing and serves as an important part of our journey.

*During the holidays, self gift with compassion, kindness, and grace.*

### TIP #6: THE RULES OF 5

Treat your senses to the Rule of 5. Your emotions are raw, but your body could use some TLC. Each day acknowledge 5 things you can see, 4 things you can feel, 3 things you can hear, 2 things you can smell, and 1 thing you can taste. Wear a soft scarf (feel). Enjoy an eggnog latte (taste). Use aromatherapy soap in the shower (smell). You get the idea. Small gestures like these offer your physical body a reminder that not all pleasure is lost and allow us to deposit small moments of joy in our hearts to help balance the sadness.

### TIP #7: WHEN THE MOOD STRIKES . . .

Feel joy without guilt. Give yourself permission, because it releases positive hormones that are good for your brain. If you find yourself humming to holiday music, don't stop. The heart can feel joy the same time as sorrow, and it helps to balance the sadness. Allow yourself to experience moments of joy without guilt. Your spirit needs it.

### TIP #8: HONOR THE PAST

Find a way to include your loved one's memory in the festivities. Hang their stocking and fill it with cat toys or dog treats to share with the family pet on Christmas morning. Visit your loved one's favorite coffee stand and pay it forward. Buy a small bouquet of balloons in your loved one's favorite color and leave it in a public spot for a stranger to find.

### TIP #9: HEAL OTHERS

Do something in the community that lifts your spirits. It induces a helper's high that's good for the brain, it's gratifying to the heart, and is a good reminder that we aren't alone in our struggles. It helps us keep perspective that the holidays can be hard for a variety of reasons, and helping others helps our own heart to heal.

### TIP #10: SEEK OUT SUPPORT.

Surround yourself with others who speak your loss language. A quick internet search will likely reveal a number of local groups led by seasoned grievers trained to hold a sacred space for your sorrow. If that isn't your style, grab one of the books in the Grief Diaries series, take a self enrichment class, or join the growing number of live Facebook events without leaving your living room. No matter how you seek support, surrounding yourself with others who speak the language of sorrow is an important part of healing.

# THE YOUNG WIDOW

While the grieving process is similar to those experiencing any loss, the content and prescription for reconciliation of young widows requires an emphasis on a number of special activities.

For many young widows, this is the first time there has been a major loss—of any kind. Until now, life was normal and predictable, filled with school, perhaps college, idyllic romance, a home, children, developing careers, and more. They had everything according to the American dream and expectation—ever onward and upward, each year better than the last.

Of course, there was nothing to prepare them to deal with major and often sudden reversal.

The statements below represent many of the feelings and concerns of women who are widowed early in their married life.

- In one moment, my life, my hopes, my dreams turned upside-down so completely.
- After years of preparation for life together with a man I admire, respect and love, I find myself overwhelmed with responsibilities and aloneness.
- I find myself with so many unsatisfied needs—physical needs, emotional needs, intellectual needs, and spiritual needs.
- I really don't know how to be a single parent. I'm scared.

### ALONENESS

There've always been people around. Father, mother, sisters and brothers, college roommates, the old high school gang, hanging out with friends, my special boyfriend, fiancée, lover, husband, and perhaps children. Now it is me alone or me and my kid(s).

No adult to talk to, to listen to me, to touch me, to take care of me, to sleep with me, for me to listen to, care about and take care of.

The world is organized for couples and I'm not part of that anymore. It is all gone, and I am alone with myself or kid(s) who are demanding of my nonexistent energy.

### PARTNER DEPENDENCY

Can I be a fulfilled woman without intimacy in my life? My social modeling has always been centered around being with a partner.

All my physical, emotional and social needs require the close presence of a partner in my life. Am I capable of attracting someone else now that I'm older and perhaps have kids?

Am I going to change my attitudes about the need for companionship? How am I going to find someone else, anyone else?

### LONELINESS

This is separate from aloneness. Aloneness is being alone and perhaps missing the adult activity I once enjoyed. But this overwhelming feeling of loneliness is separate and apart from being alone.

It is my wave of depression which may be present even when I'm at work or around others. I can feel lonely even when I'm not alone. It's just different and I'm not certain I want to go on living this way.

My loneliness really stems from my feelings of worthlessness. I've needed the company and admiration of others to feel valuable. I have lost what I had, and I am lonely.

### RESPONSIBILITY

I am a responsible person, but I never had this degree of responsibility thrust upon me before and don't know how to handle it. I'm really scared.

There is the financial concern of how I'm going to support myself and perhaps my kid(s). Just being alone and raising the children alone in this day and age is frightening.

How am I going to provide? How am I going to take care of all these possessions? How am I going to ensure proper childcare when I go back to work?

### THE UNKNOWN

What will become of me?

Will I ever love again?

Will I live the rest of my life feeling the way I do right now? If so, is it all worth it?

This decision, that decision, am I doing it correctly?

What would my partner have done?

# THE FAMILY MEETING

The family meeting process has been used successfully by family units to establish and maintain an elevated level of communication based upon honesty and openness in the disclosure of feelings. This process will work with any family unit of two or more people living together. To be effective, all persons living together under the same roof must participate; it just doesn't work if any member is excluded.

## THE FAMILY MEETING PROCESS

1. Select a sacred time that's agreeable to all family members. It is **essential** the sacred time be honored; all other family and individual activities must be planned around this time. Keeping this sacred time is a covenant by each individual which gives honor to the importance of the family unit.

2. The family meeting is held once a week at the agreed upon sacred time.

3. Family members will take turns convening the meeting. The convener will begin the meeting by sharing his/her own reality with other family members. This self-disclosure is designed to include all positive and negative feelings. For example:

    - "This is my hurt, my pain . . . "
    - "I am feeling guilty for having done . . . "
    - "I feel angry when . . . "
    - "I feel proud of myself for . . . "
    - "This is the space I am in right now . . . "

    It is extremely important that the person sharing only talk of his or her own feelings. This is not the time to talk about others, nor is this the time to lecture, preach or gripe.

4. No one is allowed to interrupt the one who is disclosing him or herself. Other family members must listen until it is their turn to share.

5. When the first person is finished sharing, the next person is not to answer or defend against feelings previously shared by another, but begins to share his or her direct feelings.

6. This process continues uninterrupted until all have shared.

7. When all family members have finished sharing, a discussion period is held only for the purpose of clarification. It is important to keep this time free from advice, argument and problem solving. Stick only to clarifying what was heard to be certain it was what the other person really meant to convey.

    - "I heard you say . . . , does that mean you were . . . ?"
    - "I didn't understand what you meant when you said . . . "
    - "Please repeat . . . I'm not sure I really understood you."

8. In the event of a disagreement or fight, no one is allowed to leave the room until an agreement has been reached which is satisfactory to all family members. Difficulties can be solved by honest conversation which honors each person's individual feelings. Fighting is not necessarily bad. If the fighting is fair, communication continues. The real enemy of communication and relating is silence.

REMEMBER:

- ☑ Never attack. Keep the focus on self, using I statements. I feel, I sense, I think, I will…
- ☑ Repeat everything you think you hear to the person who said it. "I heard you say…." Then listen for the confirmation.
- ☑ Regardless of how foreign to your own ideas and values, take everything that is said seriously. Making light of another's honest feelings is a devastating putdown.

This process is not intended to solve individual problems which are best served by qualified therapists. It is an excellent means of how to use openness and honesty to help nurture the family unit by promoting self-disclosure and the art of listening.

# MARRIAGE AFTER DEATH OF A CHILD

Don't expect your spouse to be a tower of strength when he or she is also experiencing grief. Be sensitive to your spouse's personality style. In general, he or she will approach grief with the same personality habits used in approaching life. It may be very private, very open and sharing, or some-where in between.

> **REMEMBER**
>
> Men and women are wired differently. You won't react to the loss the same way. Don't try to understand one another's way of coping, just honor it.

- Find a sympathetic friend, someone who cares and will listen without judgment or interruption.

- Do talk about your child with your spouse. If necessary, set a daily or weekly time for this.

- Seek the help of a counselor if grief or problems in your marriage are getting out of hand.

- Do not overlook or ignore anger-causing situations. It's like adding fuel to a fire—eventually there will be an explosion. Deal with things as they occur.

- Remember, you loved your spouse enough to marry. Try to keep your marriage alive by having dates or time alone together to create new memories.

- Join a support group for bereaved parents. If you are unable to attend as a couple, come by yourself or with a friend. It is a good place to learn about grief and to feel understood. Do not pressure your spouse to attend with you if it is not to his or her preference.

- Join a mutually agreeable community-betterment project as common ground between you.

- Be gentle with yourself and your mate. Have grace.

- Do not blame yourself or your mate for what you were powerless to prevent. If you blame your spouse or personally feel responsible for your child's death, seek counseling for yourself and your marriage.

- Realize that you are not alone. There are many bereaved parents who survived loss of a child.

- Choose to believe that one day your heart will again know the joys of life.

- Recognize your extreme sensitivity and vulnerability, and be alert to the tendency to take things personally.

- Read about grief, especially the books written for bereaved parents.

- Take your time with decisions about your child's things, change of residence, etc.

- Be aware of unrealistic expectations for yourself or your mate.
- Remember, there is no timetable. Everyone goes through grief differently, even parents of the same child.
- Try to remember that your spouse is doing the best he or she can.
- Marital friction is normal in any marriage. Don't blow it out of proportion.
- Try not to let little everyday irritants become major issues. Talk about them and try to be patient.
- Be sensitive to the needs and wishes of your spouse as well as yourself. Sometimes it is important to compromise.
- It is very important to keep the lines of communication open.
- Work on your grief instead of wishing that your spouse would handle his or her grief differently. You will find that you will have enough just handling your own grief. Remember, when you help yourself cope with grief, it indirectly helps your spouse.

**Value your marriage—you have lost enough.**

# PANIC ATTACKS

Panic attacks are episodes of acute fear that can appear suddenly and incapacitate without apparent cause or rational explanation. For many, it is so irrational that they are afraid to tell anyone about their incident for fear they will be judged mad, crazy, or insane. Some have described their attacks as feeling like they will faint or even die on the spot. They can't breathe, their hyperventilating, their heart is pounding like a drum, their hands are trembling, and their legs feel like jello.

Typically, a panic attack is preceded by a period of stress overload. The person experiencing it may feel generally rundown, poorly nourished for the amount of stress being carried. Frequently he or she is exercising a great deal of introspection and worry about stress-related symptoms.

Before proceeding with the strategies outlined below, it is necessary for a medical doctor, one with a good understanding of nutrition and the effect of body chemistry on the autonomic nervous system, to eliminate certain conditions which could be organic causes for episodes of panic. Let your doctor know you wish to eliminate potential causes. Take control of your body and mind. Don't permit anyone to get you into a chemical drug/medication trap without a second opinion and clear evidence of an organic problem.

### RECOVERY

This is an outline of a 7-step program utilized by the Panic Attack Sufferers Support Group (PASS). It is basic and easy to understand. It is easy to accomplish but requires a major willingness to make changes. If we continue to do the same things, we continue to get the same results. A willingness to do something different from what we currently do is necessary for this program to minimize your attacks of panic, fear and terror.

### STEP 1: DIET

- As panic attacks are often related to the body's blood sugar, eat balanced meals based on the basic four food groups. Eliminate simple sugars such as corn syrup.
- Avoid alcohol.
- Spread out your meals, eat 5 or 6 small meals each day.
- Have small amounts of protein with each meal.
- Avoid caffeine.
- Take a daily multivitamin.
- Go easy on fats and salt.

## STEP 2: RELAXATION

Relaxation is a learned skill that needs daily practice. Body chemistry changes with relaxation. Endorphins which promote good, calm feelings are produced under circumstances of relaxation, and adrenalin—which is often associated with panic and fear—is lessened. Practice diaphragmatic breathing (laughing creates the perfect diaphragmatic breath). Learn to stretch your body with slow soft stretches through tai chi or dancing. Learn progressive relaxation from audio or videos.

**Learn this quieting reflex which you can do unobtrusively anywhere, anytime.** Practice this until you can perform it instantly at times of panic onset. It really help.

- Smile inwardly. Unclench your teeth and jaw.
- Tell yourself, "My eyes are twinkling and sparkling."
- Imagine inhaling through the soles of your feet, up through your legs and into your stomach. Feel the upward flow of warmth and heaviness.
- Imagine the air flowing back down through your feet and out the soles, taking all the tension along with it. Let your jaw, tongue and shoulders go limp.

## STEP 3: EXERCISE

A regular exercise routine provides effective oxygenation of your body. It need not be overly strenuous, just regular. Try swimming, brisk walking, running in place, bike riding, rowing, dancing, jogging, rope jumping, calisthenics. Among all its other benefits, exercise also helps dissipate anger. Common sense precautions:

- Check with your doctor before beginning an exercise program.
- Don't begin if you are just recovering from a cold, flu or other illness.
- Start gradually and don't overdo it. Pace yourself. Work at a comfortable speed.
- Always begin by warming up with stretches to wake up the body and prevent injury.

## STEP 4: ATTITUDE

Letting go to be in control. Paradoxical? Yes. But it works. Learning to honor and develop your courageous self. Using positive imagery and affirmations.

## STEP 5: IMAGINATION

Be open to new situations, be open to learning. Use visualization and positive affirmations.

## STEP 6: SOCIAL SUPPORT

Network and spend time with others who speak your loss language.

## STEP 7: YOUR SPIRITUAL SIDE

Tap into your spiritual side. Get to know God better. Get to know scripture better.

# SHOULDS OR SHOULD NOTS

Following are common questions about what people should or should not do, and in what timeframe. There are no **should** or **should not** standards. Your journey through grief and the reconciliation process is unique to you. Do whatever feels right to your heart.

If the question concerns the space you personally live in, the decision is yours alone. If other family members share that space, then it is important to communicate with one another about what your needs and expectations are.

Following are common questions and suggestions.

Should I clear out my loved one's personal belongings? How soon should I be doing this?

Some people find it cathartic to handle their loved one's belongings. Others find it painful. Still others find comfort by leaving their clothes, personal items, tools, and other such stuff in place. There is no inappropriate window. As long as keeping your loved one's belongings does not involve any bizarre behavior or cause ongoing stress, there is no time limit. If these things are perceived by others as taking up space, it is your decision how you fill your space. This may upset family members who believe that they know what is best for you. Gently remind them that this is something you need to do in your own time, and you'll know when the time is right.

Should I sell my home or move to a different location?

If possible, wait to make this decision as long as it is financially reasonable to do so. The process of packing and moving adds extra stress to your life, and can distract you from your griefwork. Additionally, moving to new, unfamiliar surroundings can be very stressful for some. Changing your surroundings will not take your grief away. Your grief will move with you wherever you go. If you need to move, know that you will need additional support, emotionally and otherwise.

How regularly should I visit the cemetery?

How often you visit your loved one's final resting place is a very personal choice. Some people find comfort by doing so, and report feeling closer to their loved one. Others cannot bring themselves to go to the cemetery. Some people visit every day, even several times a day. Others feel guilty for not visiting enough, or not at all. Go if it brings you comfort. If you would like to visit and cannot do this alone, bring along a trusted friend or family member for emotional support.

Should I celebrate the upcoming holiday or my loved one's birthday?

The first birthday and holidays following a loss can be very difficult. Many people feel anything but festive, and just want the holidays to go away.

Anticipating an upcoming holiday, birthday or anniversary creates a great deal of stress for people who are grieving. Oftentimes, the anticipation of the day can be worse than the day itself. Do only what you can in the days prior.

It may be helpful to ask a friend to take care of the things that are making you feel anxious. Try not to worry about expectations of others. You do not have to take care of anyone or anything, unless you choose to do so.

If you have family traditions in which you feel you cannot host or participate, communicate your feelings to those who are involved in the festivity. If at first you feel you can participate, know that it is okay to change your mind. On the other hand, you may not accept an invitation, and when the day arrives, you feel you could go. Do what feels right to you **in the moment**. Most people will understand, and you do not have to explain yourself either way.

### I'm mad at God but afraid to admit that. Should I tell someone?

Many mourners find themselves mad at God or their church. Sometimes they even question their faith. This is more common than not. Find a spiritual mentor whom you can talk to freely, and be honest about your feelings. Chances are that you aren't the first person who has come to them with such feelings, and he or she might have sage advice that will help you process the strong emotions.

If you aren't comfortable talking to someone in your church, give it to God. He hears you, loves you, and won't strike you down for mourning so deeply. He created you as a human, with human emotions. Remember that your grief is a testament to the love you have for one of His children. He gets it. He really does.

# THE POWER OF PRAYER

Stacy Roorda, a busy 37-year-old mother of two young girls, had noticed a lump in her left armpit for some months. Having moved into a larger home the previous winter, she had long attributed the pestering symptom to the strain of moving.

Nine months later, in November 2006, Stacy finally went to see her naturopath. Suspicious of something sinister, the doctor immediately sent Stacy for a battery of tests. The results rocked her world.

She had an aggressive form of stage 4 breast cancer.

With two little girls at home, surgery was immediately scheduled to remove the primary mass in Stacy's left breast.

Then the other shoe dropped.

Pre-op labs revealed Stacy was unexpectedly expecting—and the cancer was feeding on the very hormones her unborn baby needed to survive.

**It was gloom and doom. Tears were shed, prayers were said, and she handed it over to God.**

"I immediately got an image of a harness that racecar drivers wear. The feeling was instant. 'Sit down and buckle up. It's going to be a rough road, but you'll be fine.' I grabbed onto that thought and never let go," shares Stacy.

Finding her case beyond his scope, the local oncologist sent Stacy and her husband south to Seattle.

Because the pregnancy hormone was the cancer's food source, the team of specialists offered few options. Stacy's best chance for survival depended on immediate termination of the pregnancy followed by aggressive treatment. They had no time to waste. The doctors told her it was her only hope. The cancer was too advanced.

**It was either Stacy's life, or the baby. They couldn't save both.**

Against medical advice, she refused to abort the baby. The doctors gave her three years to live at best.

News of Stacy's plight spread rapidly in her small hometown of Lynden, Washington. With a 2-year-old and 4-year-old at home, and the very lives of Stacy and her unborn child at stake, family and friends sprang into action.

Meals were brought, childcare was juggled, and a church prayer chain was started.

Stacy was known for her devout faith. And her stubbornness. Despite pressure from the best oncologists in the state, she refused to terminate the unexpected pregnancy.

An older, less effective chemotherapy deemed safer for the developing baby was planned. Nicknamed Red Death, the goal was to slow down the cancer and buy Stacy some time until the baby could be born. Treatment began immediately.

Back at home, news of the family's troubles spread. So did the prayer chain.

While bolstered by the many petitions, Stacy wasn't about to be left out of the prayer party held on her behalf.

"Before every round of chemo, I would go into the bathroom by myself. I would take a few moments to look directly at Jesus. You can always look around in the world and listen to the negative stuff, but if you look up to Jesus, that is where you find peace that surpasses all understanding. And I prayed that Jesus would fill the room with angels. I felt that as long as Jesus was there with me, I could do it," she said.

But after five rounds of Red Death, the baby started showing signs of distress. They had to stop.

Things went from bad to worse.

An MRI showed the cancer had advanced to Stacy's spine, and was marching downward. At 32 weeks gestation, they needed to deliver the baby before the cancer reached the womb.

"Once again I was totally shocked. I thought back to the image of the seat belt. I had a very serious conversation with God.

"I don't remember signing up for this part. I've done everything you asked, and I've trusted you. You brought us through and we've been lifted up in prayer by loved ones and complete strangers around the world. How could this be?"

"Once again, I got the feeling God was indeed there and would bring me through it. He gave me a peace that surpassed all understanding, all I had to do was keep praying," she said.

By this time, reports of Stacy's dire situation had spread far and wide.

"I heard that my story reached missionaries, and that people all around the world were praying. That was the most humbling part, is that people were praying for me who had never met me. That is what carried Matt and I through the whole thing," she said.

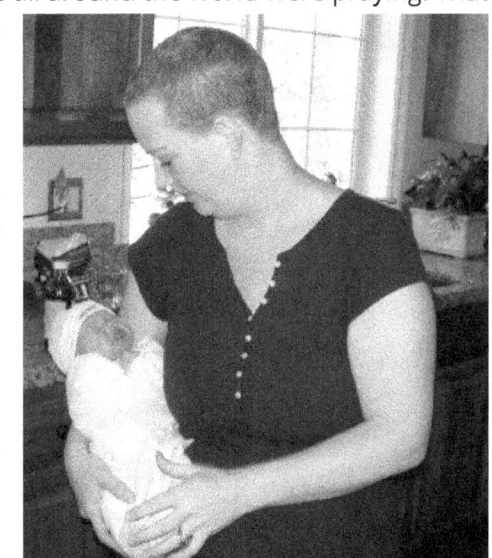

With news that such a premature delivery was imminent, the prayers that surrounded Stacy and her family took on a new urgency.

Less than 48 hours later, Jazmine Stacy Roorda was born.

Weighing just 3.5 pounds and lacking the sucking reflex that hadn't yet developed, their new daughter was otherwise perfect.

The announcement of the baby's birth spread along the prayer chain, but the petitions on their behalf didn't stop.

With the pregnancy behind her, two young daughters at home, a preemie in the NICU, Stacy now faced the cancer treatment head on.

The intensity of the prayer chain that now stretched around the world fortified Stacy's determination. She believed without a doubt that the positive, loving energy contained in a prayer chain is a force that cannot be denied.

What happened next is what some might call a miracle: the treatment designed to buy Stacy a bit more time with her family instead, and inexplicably, brought the cancer to a standstill. It hasn't budged since.

Fast forward thirteen years. Against the odds, Stacy not only survived the doctors' prognosis, so did her baby.

With bone mets, Stacy will never be free from cancer. But for reasons doctors can't explain, it inexplicably fossilized in the various parts of her body.

Stacy gives much of the credit to the prayers that came from strangers across the globe.

What is prayer? It's love in an energetic form. Many use it to talk to God. Others use it to spread light in the world.

No matter how you use or label it, it's a powerful energy, love in its purest form.

"The power of prayer is how God works in this world, through people and their petition. Their desire to pray for a complete stranger is out of their love for Jesus. Love trumps everything," she says.

Stacy Roorda is aware that skeptics are still waiting for proof in the power of prayer. But it doesn't faze her.

The prayer party that spanned the world on her behalf is all the proof she needs.

STACY ROORDA WITH DAUGHTERS HANNAH, ZOE AND JAZMINE (2019)

WATCH CHURCH VIDEO: https://vimeo.com/82251139

# FOR MY COMPASSIONATE FRIENDS

BY MARILYN ROLLINS
The Compassionate Friends
Lake-Porter County, Indiana

How is it that I know you?
How'd you get into my life?
Sometimes when I look at you,
It cuts me like a knife.

I do not want to know you,
I don't want to cross that line.
Let's both go back into the past,
When everything was fine.

You've held me and you've hugged me,
And dried a tear or two,
Yet, you're practically a stranger,
Why do you do the things you do?

Of course, I know the reason,
We are in this club we're in,
And why we hold on to each other
Like we are long lost kin.

For us to know each other,
We had to lose a kid,
I wish I'd never met you,
But, I'm so thankful that I did.

# THE WAILING TENT

Dear grieving mother,

Welcome to the sisterhood of the wailing tent. With profound condolences, I know you'll soon forget my greeting, for your heart and soul have sustained a terrible blow.

The shock known as "the fog" will accompany you for some time, greatly impacting your memory. So I offer you this written welcome to refer to when your recollection falters.

The wailing tent is an honored place where only mothers with a broken spirit can enter. Admittance is gained not with an ID card bearing your name, but with the fresh sorrow etched on your heart.

Membership is free, for you have already paid the unfathomable price.

Directions to the wailing tent are secret, available only to mothers who speak our language of everlasting grief.

No rules are posted, no hours are noted. There's no hierarchy or governing body. Your membership has no expiration date, it is lifelong.

The refuge offered within its walls does not judge members based on age, religious belief, or social status. Hang your mask outside, and if you can't make it past the door, we will surround you with love right where you lay.

The wailing tent is a shelter where mothers shed anguished tears among her newfound sisters. A haven where all forms of wailing are honored, understood, and accepted.

In the beginning, you will be very afraid, and will hate the wailing tent and everything it stands for. You will flail, thrash about, and spew vile words in protest. You will fight to be free of the walls, wishing desperately to offer a plea bargain for a different tent, learn a different language. Those emotions will last for some time. Your family and friends cannot accompany you here. The needs of the wailing tent are invisible to them. Though they'll try, they simply cannot understand the disembodied, guttural howls heard within.

In the beginning, your stays here will seem endless. Over time, the need for your visits will change and eventually you will observe some mothers talking, even smiling, rather than wailing. Those mothers have learned to balance profound anguish with moments of peace, though they still need to seek refuge among us from time to time.

Do not judge those mothers as callused or strong, for they have endured profound heartache to attain the peace they have found. Their visits here are greatly valued, for their hard-earned wisdom offers hope that we, too, will learn to balance the sadness in our hearts.

Lastly, you need not flash your ID card or introduce yourself each time you visit, for we know who you are. You are one of us, an honorary lifelong sister of the wailing tent.

Welcome, my wailing sister.

LYNDA CHELDELIN FELL (2014)

> **Grief is learning to live with your loved one in your heart instead of your arms.**
>
> LYNDA CHELDELIN FELL

# RESOURCES

## ONLINE SUPPORT

### ICARE GRIEF SUPPORT WEB PORTAL

The iCare website of grief resources available to families 24/7.

$49/MONTHLY  |  ICAREGRIEFSUPPORT.COM

### CUSTOM GRIEF SUPPORT WEB PORTAL

A custom website of grief resources available to families 24/7.

$69/MONTHLY  |  ICAREGRIEFSUPPORT.COM

---

## TRAINING RESOURCES

### ICARE GRIEF SUPPORT GROUP FACILITATOR MANUAL

From start to finish, everything you need to run a Christ-centered grief support group for your community and congregants. Manual can be used multiple times. 8.5x11"  |  220 pgs  |  full color

$79.95  |  ICAREGRIEFSUPPORT.COM/SUPPORTGROUPS

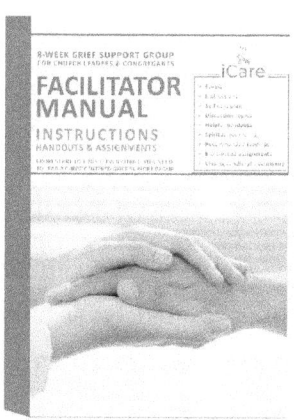

### ICARE GRIEF SUPPORT GROUP PARTICIPANT WORKBOOK

Includes discussion topics, self-care tips, Bible assignments, spiritual journaling, activities and more. 8.5x11"  |  188 pgs  |  full color

$24.95  |  ICAREGRIEFSUPPORT.COM/SUPPORTGROUPS

## LITERATURE & BOOKS

### RESILIENCE RX™ – ONE SHEETS

Resilience Rx™ promotes evidence-based self-help techniques and positive coping strategies that support mourners through loss. Each one-sheet is a snapshot of the science behind the technique and how to implement it after loss.

Sold in packs of 10. Size 8.5x11"

1. Chromotherapy
2. Dance/Movement Therapy
3. Forest Therapy
4. Hug Therapy
5. Laugh Therapy
6. Sensorial Therapy
7. Holiday Tips
8. Insomnia after loss

P07 | $15/10-PACK | ICAREGRIEFSUPPORT.COM/RESILIENCE

### ICARE PLANNING GUIDE

Filled with helpful prompts, the iCare™ Planning Guide is an easy-to-do form-based guide that helps clients decide and document their own funeral wishes. Measures 8.5 x 11, 22 pages. Sold in packs of 10.

P08 | $49/PACK | ICAREGRIEFSUPPORT.COM/PLANNING

## ICARE BOOKLET SERIES

The iCare™ Series offers easy reading and helpful support for your families delivered directly to their door. The books are designed to be read at 1, 3, 6 and 11 months during the first year of grief plus a special holiday booklet filled with tips for coping.

- One set of 5 booklets mailed to your families at 1, 3, 6, 11 months after loss plus a bonus holiday booklet
- Simple reading
- Helpful tips
- No minimum order

OPTION 1: Give as a gift of understanding to your families
$14.95/SET   |   ICAREGRIEFSUPPORT.COM/BOOKLETS


OPTION 2: Mailing service with custom imprint with your return address
$24/SET   |   ICAREGRIEFSUPPORT.COM/BOOKLETS

## GRIEF DIARIES AWARD-WINNING ANTHOLOGY SERIES

### GRIEF DIARIES: SURVIVING LOSS OF A CHILD

Surviving Loss of a Child shares the poignant journeys of 22 women as they search for healing and hope after losing a child. Exploring how each mother faced a journey they couldn't fathom, **Surviving Loss of a Child** offers comfort and hope and is a reminder to others who find themselves facing the same journey that they can survive. Foreword by Grieving Men's R. Glenn Kelly.

MSRP $16.95  |  CHURCH PRICE $8.00/ea  |  ISBN: 978-1944328009
shop.alybluemedia.com/products/childws

### GRIEF DIARIES: THROUGH THE EYES OF A WIDOW

**Through the Eyes of a Widow** is a collection of tender stories by widows as they learned to adapt after losing her husband. Each shares the challenges, where she found the most help, and the hope she found along the way.

MSRP $16.95  |  CHURCH PRICE $8.00/ea  |  ISBN: 978-1944328641
shop.alybluemedia.com/products/widowws

### GRIEF DIARIES: SURVIVING LOSS OF A SPOUSE

**Surviving Loss of a Spouse** features the poignant journeys of 15 men and women as they move through the aftermath of losing a husband or wife. Each narration offers a firsthand account of how each widow and widower faced the funeral, handled his or her spousal belongings, navigated the year of firsts, and how each fought to find hope in the aftermath. Foreword by award-winning playwright Carol Scibelli, author of Poor Widow Me.

MSRP $14.95  |  CHURCH PRICE $6.50/ea  |  ISBN: 978-1944328016
shop.alybluemedia.com/products/spousews

# iCARE™ GRIEF MINISTRY GUIDE

### GRIEF DIARIES: SURVIVING LOSS OF A PARENT

Whether one loses a parent in the natural order of life or it occurs much earlier than expected, the emotional aftermath can challenge our fears, familial relations, and even our sense of self. **Surviving Loss of a Parent** offers 17 firsthand accounts that yields a powerful look at how such losses can influence every aspect of our life. Foreword by radio host and author Christine Duminiak.

MSRP $14.95   |   CHURCH PRICE $5.50/ea   |   ISBN: 978-1944328078

shop.alybluemedia.com/products/parentws

### GRIEF DIARIES: SURVIVING LOSS OF A SIBLING

Losing a sibling is a heartbreak that leaves a hole in the fabric of every family. Facing a challenging journey that's often ignored cast into the shadows behind the bereaved parents, struggling through such emotions can be devastating lonely, **Surviving Loss of a Sibling** features the stories of 13 sisters and brothers as they fight to find the meaning of life without a sister or brother. Foreword by Benjamin Scott Allen.

MSRP $14.95   |   CHURCH PRICE $5.50/EA   |   ISBN: 978-1944328023

shop.alybluemedia.com/products/siblingws

### GRIEF DIARIES: THROUGH THE EYES OF MEN

Breaking the man code and offering readers an inside look into the hidden world of male grief, Through the Eyes of Men features the stories of 14 men of different ages who tackle the tender subject of male bereavement from the very moment their lives changed with a loved one's death. Foreword by Glen Lord, past president of the national board of directors of The Compassionate Friends.

MSRP $15.95   |   CHURCH PRICE $7.00/ea   |   ISBN: 978-1944328481

shop.alybluemedia.com/products/menws

## GRIEF DIARIES: SURVIVING LOSS BY SUICIDE

Three-time medalist, **Surviving Loss by Suicide** examines the aftermath of losing a loved one to suicide from the perspective of 12 different people. Voicing their thoughts and emotions through the funeral and beyond, each writer offers a candid look at a taboo journey. Foreword by award-winning author and suicide prevention advocate Emily Barnhardt.

MSRP $15.95   |   CHURCH PRICE $6.50/ea   |   ISBN: 978-1944328030

shop.alybluemedia.com/products/suicidews

## GRIEF DIARIES: SURVIVING LOSS BY OVERDOSE

**Surviving Loss by Overdose** is a compilation of stories by 12 people who answered 18 questions about losing a loved one to overdose in hopes of raising awareness, educating, and inviting society to offer survivors the compassion that's often denied in a stigmatized death. Forward by Elaine M. Faulkner, SUDP.

MSRP $16.95   |   CHURCH PRICE $9.00/ea   |   ISBN: 978-1950712076

shop.alybluemedia.com/products/overdosews

## GRIEF DIARIES: SURVIVING SUDDEN LOSS

**Surviving Sudden Loss** is a collection of 14 stories by parents, spouses, siblings, children, and grandparents who share their own personal insight into the hidden and often unspoken challenges of unexpectedly losing a loved one, including the emotional, mental, physical and social shifts they're forced to reckon with in the aftermath. With poignant narration, each writer shares the truth of their loss, where they found the most support, and how they rebuilt their lives in the aftermath. Coauthored by Maryann Mueller.

MSRP $18.95   |   CHURCH PRICE $9.00/ea   |   ISBN: 978-1944328894

shop.alybluemedia.com/products/suddenws

### GRIEF DIARIES: SURVIVING LOSS BY CANCER

**Surviving Loss by Cancer** offers inspiring true stories about caring for a loved one with cancer all the way through to their final breath, and beyond. Filled with compassion and under-standing, the collection of stories serve as a life raft in the storm of emotions, and offer readers hope, strength, courage after losing a loved one to cancer. Foreword by hospice director Dana Brothers.

MSRP $15.95   |   CHURCH PRICE $7.50/ea   |   ISBN:  978-1944328818

shop.alybluemedia.com/products/cancerws

### GRIEF DIARIES: SURVIVING LOSS BY IMPAIRED DRIVING

A silver medalist in the 2016 USA Best Book Awards, **Loss by Impaired Driving** examines the journeys of 17 men and women who lost one or more loved ones to a drunk, drugged or impaired driver. A must read for young, new drivers and for AA groups. Foreword by Candace Lightner, founder of MADD.

MSRP $15.95   |   CHURCH PRICE $7.00/ea   |   ISBN:  978-1944328269

shop.alybluemedia.com/products/impaired

### GRIEF DIARIES: SURVIVING LOSS BY HOMICIDE

**Surviving Loss by Homicide** shares personal accounts of coping with a violent tragedy, and sheds insight into the strength needed to stay afloat in the aftermath of intense heartache and rollercoaster of emotions ranging from shock, anger, sadness and disbelief to healing and hope. Foreword by radio host Lady Justice.

MSRP $15.95   |   CHURCH PRICE $6.50/ea   |   ISBN:  978-1944328146

shop.alybluemedia.com/products/homicidews

## EVENTS
### THE GRIEF CRUISES
www.TheGriefCruises.com

**Join us for the trip of a lifetime and leave with a lifetime of hope.**

A grief cruise is more than sharing tears and precious memories. It's filled with special moments, inspirational workshops, and new friendships that will last for life.

Seven days of respite, healing and hope, now in its fourth year of sailing, **The Grief Cruise** is a journey aboard an award-winning Royal Caribbean cruise ship.

Offering all the amenities of a 5-star cruise, The Grief Cruise features presenters, workshops, a memorial walk, creative activities and an optional burial at sea. Go for the trip of a lifetime and leave with a lifetime of hope.

> "So much compassion, overall one of the greatest and most helpful 7 days I have ever experienced in my entire life."
> -Anna

> "You gave me my first week of peace in 7 years."
> –Jane

> "I lost my 17-year-old daughter to suicide 2 years ago. The cruise has been very healing."
> –Lisa

> "What a great way to heal. The trip was fabulous and the seminars were small enough to connect and share experiences. The presenters were so sweet and gave excellent advice."
> -Melanie

## EVENTS
### THE GRIEF CRUISES

www.TheGriefCruises.com

**Join us for the trip of a lifetime and leave with a lifetime of hope.**

A grief cruise is more than sharing tears and precious memories. It's filled with special moments, inspirational workshops, and new friendships that will last for life.

Seven days of respite, healing and hope, now in its fourth year of sailing, **The Grief Cruise** is a journey aboard an award-winning Royal Caribbean cruise ship.

Offering all the amenities of a 5-star cruise, The Grief Cruise features presenters, workshops, a memorial walk, creative activities and an optional burial at sea. Go for the trip of a lifetime and leave with a lifetime of hope.

"So much compassion, overall one of the greatest and most helpful 7 days I have ever experienced in my entire life."
-Anna

"You gave me my first week of peace in 7 years."
–Jane

"I lost my 17-year-old daughter to suicide 2 years ago. The cruise has been very healing."
–Lisa

"What a great way to heal. The trip was fabulous and the seminars were small enough to connect and share experiences. The presenters were so sweet and gave excellent advice."
-Melanie

## GRIEF DIARIES: SURVIVING LOSS BY CANCER

**Surviving Loss by Cancer** offers inspiring true stories about caring for a loved one with cancer all the way through to their final breath, and beyond. Filled with compassion and under-standing, the collection of stories serve as a life raft in the storm of emotions, and offer readers hope, strength, courage after losing a loved one to cancer. Foreword by hospice director Dana Brothers.

MSRP $15.95   |   CHURCH PRICE $7.50/ea   |   ISBN:  978-1944328818

shop.alybluemedia.com/products/cancerws

## GRIEF DIARIES: SURVIVING LOSS BY IMPAIRED DRIVING

A silver medalist in the 2016 USA Best Book Awards, **Loss by Impaired Driving** examines the journeys of 17 men and women who lost one or more loved ones to a drunk, drugged or impaired driver. A must read for young, new drivers and for AA groups. Foreword by Candace Lightner, founder of MADD.

MSRP $15.95   |   CHURCH PRICE $7.00/ea   |   ISBN:  978-1944328269

shop.alybluemedia.com/products/impaired

## GRIEF DIARIES: SURVIVING LOSS BY HOMICIDE

**Surviving Loss by Homicide** shares personal accounts of coping with a violent tragedy, and sheds insight into the strength needed to stay afloat in the aftermath of intense heartache and rollercoaster of emotions ranging from shock, anger, sadness and disbelief to healing and hope. Foreword by radio host Lady Justice.

MSRP $15.95   |   CHURCH PRICE $6.50/ea   |   ISBN:  978-1944328146

shop.alybluemedia.com/products/homicidews

## NATIONAL RESOURCES

**GRIEF DIARIES**
A vast collection of stories about surviving loss.
griefdiaries.com

**ICARE GRIEF SUPPORT**
Full circle programs for the funeral and bereavement industry.
www.icaregriefsupport.com

**WHEN YOU LOSE SOMEONE**
A healing connection for all.
www.whenyoulosesomeone.com

**ELLIES WAY**
A nonprofit organization serving bereaved parents, grandparents and siblings.
www.elliesway.org

**OUTSIDE WALLS**
Resources and a ministry blog by Rev. Roland H. Johnson III.
www.outsidewalls.org

**WIDOWLUTION**
An organization dedicated to supporting widows.
widowlution.com

**THE WIDOWERS SUPPORT NETWORK**
An organization dedicated to helping widowers heal.
widowerssupportnetwork.com

**OPEN TO HOPE**
A nonprofit organization dedicated to helping people find hope after loss.
www.OpentoHope.com

**NATIONAL ALLIANCE FOR GRIEVING CHILDREN**
A nonprofit organization dedicated to serving bereaved children.
childrengrieve.org

**TAPS**
A nonprofit organization dedicated to helping families who lost a military member.
www.taps.org

**MISS FOUNDATION**
An organization dedicated to supporting people after loss.
missfoundation.org

**SOARING SPIRITS INTERNATIONAL**
An organization dedicated to supporting widows.
www.soaringspirits.org

# ACKNOWLEDGEMENTS

**Trust in the Lord with all your heart and lean not on your own understanding; in all your ways submit to him, and he will make your paths straight.**

PROVERBS 3:5-6

Lynda Cheldelin Fell is founding partner of the International Grief Institute and international bestselling author of over 35 books including the award-winning Grief Diaries series. Certified in critical incident stress management, Lynda is a national educator dedicated to setting the gold standard for quality and ethical practices in bereavement care. A member of the teaching faculty at Whatcom Community College, she teaches professional development workshops and certifications across the nation. Now considered a pioneer in resilience best practice strategies, Lynda has earned five national literary awards and five national advocacy award nominations for her work. lynda@internationalgriefinstitute.com

Linda Findlay has worked with grieving families for over twenty-six years. After losing her daughter in 1989, she started a resource and referral service for grieving families and then created personalized aftercare solutions for hundreds of funeral homes across the nation. A Christian lay counselor, Findlay is full partner of the International Grief Institute and creator of The Grief Cruises. She is an aftercare specialist who has created, facilitated, and coordinated hundreds of workshops, services, and support groups.
linda@internationalgriefinstitute.com

Rev. Roland H. Johnson III is an ordained minister and a retired sociology professor with a substantial background in academia, sociology and religious publications. He is past head of Sociology at Blinn College in Texas, and was a member of the teaching faculty at Texas A&M University and Texas State University. Now Honorary Chaplain of the Galveston Police Department, he served as both a crime victim liaison and as Head Chaplain for a number of years. Johnson holds multiple certifications and memberships including the American Sociological Association and International Conference of Police Chaplains. rolandhjohnsoniii@att.net

# PRAYER OF FAITH

UNKNOWN

We trust that beyond absence there is a presence.

That beyond the pain there can be healing.

That beyond the brokenness there can be wholeness.

That beyond the anger there may be peace.

That beyond the hurting there may be forgiveness.

That beyond the silence there may be the word.

That beyond the word there may be understanding.

That through understanding there is love.

PUBLISHED BY ALYBLUE MEDIA
www.AlyBlueMedia.com